Heroes, Heroines & Holidays

PLAYS FOR JEWISH YOUTH

BY ELAINE REMBRANDT

are Alternatives in Religious Education, Inc.
Denver, Colorado

© Copyright Alternatives in Religious Education, Inc. 1981

ALTERNATIVES IN RELIGIOUS EDUCATION, INC.
3945 South Oneida Street
Denver, Colorado 80237

Library of Congress Catalog Card Number
81-67027   ISBN 0-86705-002-0

Printed in the United States of America

ACKNOWLEDGMENTS

I would like to express my deepest appreciation to my friend and colleague, Rabbi Daniel A. Roberts, for his guidance and encouragement; to our founding rabbi, Rabbi Alan S. Green, for his love and support of creativity; to Sylvia Abrams and Sophie Herman, our present and former Educational Directors, for allowing me complete freedom to create; to my typist, Peggy Prior, for rushing to meet deadlines; and to my dear husband and children who have acted as my sounding boards with the utmost of patience.

TABLE OF CONTENTS

FOREWORD vii

INTRODUCTION ix

OH GOD, MY GOD! 1
    A Play for the High Holy
    Days, Passover or Anytime

AND BRINGS US TO THIS SEASON:
A THANKSGIVING PLAY 15
    A Play About Giving Thanks
    and the Elderly

THE SACRIFICE 25
    A Chanukah Play

GOD'S WIDE SPACES 39
    A Play for Tu B'Shvat
    or Anytime

PURIMSPIEL 53
    A Purim Musical

THE FREEDOM BIRDS 71
    A Passover Tale

FROM FREEDOM TO INDEPENDENCE . . 81
    A Presentation for Passover
    or Yom HaAtzma'ut

SO YOUNG TO DIE:
THE STORY OF HANNAH SENESH . . . 89
    A Play for Yom HaAtzma'ut
    or Yom HaShoah

STRANGER IN THE LAND:
THE STORY OF RUTH 105
    A Play for Shavuot
    or Anytime

AMOS, MAN FROM TEKOAH 119
    A Presentation for All
    Occasions

HOME TO STAY 129
    A Play for Tisha B'Av,
    Yom HaAtzma'ut or
    Yom Yerushalayim

BIBLIOGRAPHY 145

FOREWORD

We in religious education constantly search for one or two special events which will make our school year a stand out. Before you is a book of plays which will provide that additional spark. I, personally, have seen the glow in the eyes of a young actor after being in one of these productions. I know that she/he will never forget the character whose part she/he has portrayed. What is more, these performances have been an excellent vehicle for us to bind the school and congregation together. Not only have the plays been performed during religious school hours, but many of them have added "*ruach*" to Shabbat services as pulpit productions.

Elaine Rembrandt, the author of *Heroes, Heroines and Holidays* has been in charge of drama at Temple Emanu El Religious School, Cleveland, Ohio, for the last eight years. She is a speech and drama teacher by training who is well known in the Cleveland area as an actress in her own right. These scripts were developed by Elaine out of our need for material that would be both rich in content and entertaining to the audience. Their themes demonstrate how dramatics can be used as an educational tool in the Jewish school setting. Since the publication of existing material has been almost nil, we are sure that what has filled a void in our school will do the same for yours.

Although these plays were written for a congregational school, their clear messages and simple staging make them quite fitting for the informal atmosphere of camps and/or use by club groups and Jewish Community Centers.

We at Temple Emanu El know that the production of these plays in your particular institution will add zest to a class or performance group. Each play teaches the participants something about our Jewish heritage while they prepare for their roles. Audiences, whether students, parents or members of the congregation, will learn through the medium of drama about aspects of our tradition.

לא המדרש הוא העקר אלא המעשה.
(פרקי אבות א)

"The story alone is not the essence, but the action"--on with the show!

       Sylvia F. Abrams,
       Educational Director
       Temple Emanu El Religious School
       Cleveland, Ohio

18 Adar II, 5741   March 24, 1981

INTRODUCTION

The original plays in this volume are suitable for presentation by religious schools, Day Schools, camps, Jewish Community Centers, junior and senior youth groups as well as other organizations and clubs of Jewish young people.

Whatever the setting, the task of the play director is not an easy one. We are expected to find material that is both educational and exciting for both actor and audience. We are supposed to know each student well enough to cast a show intelligently with the minimum of preparation and rehearsal. It is up to us to produce a set with little technical assistance and to create beautiful costumes with very little budget. In many cases, we must also type, ditto, telephone, soothe, sew, hammer, paint and compete with basketball, Bar and Bat Mitzvah and birthday parties. But somehow the show goes on! Who says miracles don't happen anymore?

The plays in this collection will help you to accomplish more readily the goal of educating audience and actor. You will be able to produce them with the minimum of difficulty and in a brief period of time. Each play can be rehearsed during class time with the addition of two or three intensive rehearsals. These extra rehearsals, each lasting approximately two hours, are needed to work for pacing and unity of production.

The playing time for most of the plays is between 15 and 20 minutes, an ideal length for school age audiences or for pulpit presentations during services. Because the productions require little scenery, they are not cumbersome or costly to produce. In a few instances, lighting is needed to create special effects or to indicate scene changes. Some of the scripts can accommodate large groups of participants through the use of a chorus or crowd scenes. In this way everyone can have something to say. The size of the chorus or crowd can grow as further parts are needed.

Each play is preceded by a few helpful production notes. The following brief overview deals with some of the essentials of play production, including casting, blocking, pacing, sets and costumes, music and rehearsing.

Casting

After selecting your play, the next major task is casting it. Since we see our students so infrequently, how do we get to know them well enough to cast intelligently? Even among the most practiced directors, this is quite often a matter of intuition and intelligent guessing.

At your first meeting, find ways to get the children up on their feet and talking. Have them repeat simple nursery rhymes, tongue twisters or count using various emotions. This will be sufficient to allow you to identify the various voice qualities in the group. Is there someone with a mature enough voice to portray the mother? A small child? A general? If you have time at this session, you can introduce a book of oral readings, or you can save this for next time. Listen for volume, vocal range, expression and interpretation. Don't rule someone out just because of hesitant reading. A poor reader can sometimes be excellent on stage with memorized lines.

Now you are ready to bring the actual script to class. Assign parts for a general read through. This will acquaint the students with the story line and with the available parts. You will need to stop frequently to ask questions about the subject matter, or to explain the events which form the basis for the play or even to define certain words with which some students may not be familiar. Don't take anything for granted. Quite often a poor reading of a line or lines is simply due to a lack of understanding.

Before the casting is finished, give everyone a chance to read for desired parts. No student should feel that he or she was not given a fair chance to try out. The tryout selection need not be more than a short paragraph. Even young students realize that there is limited time and that no one person can monopolize the class period.

While the actual casting of the show is exciting for those given major parts, it is sometimes heartbreaking for those who are disappointed. Dealing with these traumatic experiences is also a part of your responsibility as teacher-director. Be aware that student reactions will vary from indifference to belligerence. How do you surmount this? Fortunately, everyone can participate in the play in some manner or another. A discussion with them, in very professional tones, about each actor's contribution to the production helps ease the situation. I emphasize that although some parts are larger than others, all parts are necessary to the show, and that all the actors must be serious in their treatment of the parts they are playing. "Think about your part," I tell them. "Who are you? What is your relationship with the other people in your scene?" And most important, "--react to what is going on around you!"

Blocking

Blocking is a term used to indicate any directed movement of the actors on the stage. Entrances, exits, crosses, turns, sitting, standing and the like are all considered blocking.

The blocking and your entire conception of the play should be well thought out in advance of rehearsals. In most of the plays in this collection, I have indicated blocking; however, do not feel bound to use my stage directions. These worked well for us and were appropriate for our facilities. The use of good stage directions and the use of movement are essential in order to keep a play from becoming boring to the viewer. Since your student actors are generally not experienced enough to invent on their own, the stage directions and use of movement must be the director's responsibility. Students do now and then have creative thoughts so it's a good idea to listen to all suggestions. The key word to staging as well as line delivery is *variety!* Don't be afraid to let your imagination run wild (as long as it doesn't pose any danger to the actors--I draw the line at hanging from the drapery rod!). Learn to utilize every entry and architectural structure in the room! For example, in the play, "The Freedom Birds" (see page 71), the birds are perched on top of the railings which divide the *bimah* from the congregation. If using a proscenium stage, some scenes can be played in front of the curtain to hide a scene change, or as a preliminary to another scene.

Audiences are always delighted when actors enter through the audience or from unexpected places. Use stairs to the stage level for entrances and exits from the audience. Make sure that you differentiate between outdoor and indoor accesses in the same play so as not to confuse your audience. Use ladders and platforms on the stage or performing area to give dimension and variety, especially in a presentational kind of production. Let your actors sit on the edge of the stage (as long as they can be seen), lean against the proscenium arch, face upstage (as long as they can be heard), and even use the curtain as a prop! In one production we did, heads popped out of the middle opening of the curtain at different heights, as well as along the floor line. It was startling, exciting and very effective.

Pacing

The rhythm of line delivery and cue pick up also require variation to be effective. The importance of pacing is not just to keep the audience from becoming bored listening to the actors, but to create the desired effect or emotional response on the part of the audience. The most effective tool in creating these desired effects is the *dramatic pause*. It's too bad it can't be packaged and sold. I would buy a gross! "Here, Billy, is a box of Dramatic Pauses. I want you to take one out and use it every once in a while." Ah, well! Instead, you will have to direct them into the script whenever you feel it necessary. They can create tension, comedy, pathos--the effects are myriad.

There is nothing more deadly than long periods of silence during the dialogue of a play while the actors and the audience wait for someone to make an entrance. Actors must be directed to anticipate their entrances so that they are in place and ready to deliver their lines on cue! Silence, like action, should occur only when it is directed into a play. In a well paced show, the actors pick up their cues and all entrances are made with no interminable waits, without an actor or actress too obviously assuming a blocked position, with variety in line delivery and with effective use of the dramatic pause.

Sets and Costumes

Ah, ah, ah! Don't throw anything away indiscriminately! You might be able to use it or make it into something for one of your shows. Boxes, cartons, crates, remnant fabric, old jewelry and long dresses and shirts can always be used. Save, Save, Save! Beg or borrow a closet or cupboard where you can store your accumulation of costumes. Develop a wardrobe inventory so that each new production does not necessitate a complete new costume search. Make sure that everyone at your synagogue knows that you are in charge of the costumes, and that nobody is allowed to take them for any reason without first checking with you and signing out for each specific item.

For sets you will, of course, be limited by the kind of area in which you will produce your play. A proscenium stage with a traveling curtain will allow for more variety of effect than floor level productions. But your only limitation is your imagination! Ask your neighborhood appliance dealer for empty refrigerator boxes. Different scenes can be painted on opposite sides of these and--presto!--you can change the scene by merely turning the box around.

It's especially wise to create items that can be saved and revised over the years. Trees can be used over and over again to indicate any outdoor scene. A window flat can be redressed in different fabrics play after play to become the backdrop of many indoor scenes. Other staples are a small wooden table (the main fixture of a Sabbath play when draped with a white lace cloth and decorated with a centerpiece and candlesticks) and several low stools. Make a note of when each item was made and where it is being stored so that you can find it readily when it is needed again. It's a good idea to keep an updated list of all properties and set items and costumes in the synagogue office. Such a record will really be helpful to any other director who needs to know what inventory there is with which to work.

Pulpit presentations performed during a regular worship service are designed to use nothing more than a table and chairs or perhaps a couple of easily moved trees. When performing on the pulpit, the stage cannot be preset. It is also too time consuming and cumbersome to set anything more elaborate than a few props on stage. For this type of play it is best to rely on colorful costuming for your effects.

Over the years we have accumulated a nice assortment of basic robes in many different colors and patterns which fill the bill for most biblical plays. You might enlist the aid of a few parents who are talented with a needle and thread to produce some basic costumes for you. It's a good idea to prowl the fabric shops for remnant pieces which might be just the right size for a child's robe. You might not need it right at that moment. But if the fabric is interesting and the price is right, buy it and hang on to it for just the right occasion. Old pieces of drapery or upholstery material make wonderful throws for the throne of Ahashuerus or Pharaoh. Our Jewish Community Center has a wonderful theatre group and is most generous about loaning costumes. Check out your Sisterhood's rummage sale. Sometimes you will find leftover items that would be perfect for costumes.

Music

I love music! And so does the audience, whether it is live or taped. I have found that music can set a mood when nothing else can--especially if you don't have stage lighting. Some taped music to open the show or to act as background to a reading can do a lot to enhance the production. Be certain that it is just the right sound and length and that it does not distract from the speaker or the action.

Rehearsing

The first rehearsal session is a good time to discuss goals and objectives, to hand out performance dates and to try to discern the abilities and talents of the group. It is very important to send home the schedule of performance dates as soon as possible. If additional rehearsals are needed, that schedule, too, should be handed out as early as possible. Thus you can learn of possible conflicts and, if necessary, other outside activities may be rescheduled to fit the rehearsal schedule.

You may wish to schedule additional rehearsals on the days your younger students attend midweek Hebrew classes at the synagogue. For junior and senior high school students, early evening rehearsals may be best because of their involvement in sports and other after school activities.

Schedule rehearsals so that there is a minimum of wasted time for each student. Assemble performers by scenes as in the following example:

        4:00 - 4:45   Scene 1
        4:45 - 5:15   Scene 2

Or you can schedule some time with individual principal players to go over a lengthy speech or a bit of blocking.

Energy

Probably the most important element that you, as the director, can introduce into any play is *energy!* The only way I have ever found of creating energy among my actors (many of whom would rather be spending the morning in bed) is by working on a high energy level myself. I interact constantly with the players during rehearsals. Don't be afraid to get right up there on the stage. Show them how to walk or sit or stand like an old person or how to move with the regal bearing of a king. Many directors think it is taboo to say a line for, or show, an actor or actress how he or she wishes it to be interpreted. This may be the case for seasoned performers. With fledgling actors, however, imitation is often the best way to instruct.

And don't forget, we are working against time. We don't have the luxury of waiting for the dawn to come up like thunder--we have to make it happen! When you need to stimulate and loosen up your actors, don't hesitate to stop right in the middle of a rehearsal and organize some group body and vocal exercises. Energy levels seem to diminish as a scene is rehearsed over and over. Such exercises often get things moving again. They also represent a good way of involving those individuals who are not rehearsing at the moment.

It is my hope that the plays included in this volume will be as interesting to stage and as fun to produce as they have been for me and my classes. No other experience can quite match the feeling of pride and accomplishment actors feel when they hear that magic sound of appreciative applause. It's hard work, but worth it. Break a leg!

Oh God, My God!

Grades 7-12

PRODUCTION NOTES

It works well to perform this play on the *bimah* in modern dress. Dress male angels in suits and ties and the girl angel in a skirt and blazer with a ribbon tied at the neck of her blouse. All can wear identical wigs made from the white bathing caps used for racing. Cover these with cotton balls until puffy, then sprinkle with sparkles. Make an identifying badge for each angel: peace, love, truth and right (righteousness won't fit on a badge). Adam and Eve can wear running shorts and T-shirts (in opposite colors with their names lettered on the front), tube socks and tennis shoes. Moses can be dressed completely in western style and can even speak with a slight twang. The gentlemen of the Jerusalem Political Club might wear formal looking suits or tuxedos with the women in dressy dresses, lots of jewelry and even some borrowed fur stoles.

God is never seen, but His "entrance" at the beginning can be made humorous by playing on a tape recorder the sound of a door opening and closing followed by footsteps. The angels should be blocked to "watch Him come down the center aisle," indicating His closeness by a nod of their heads.

Whenever there is a scene during which only the voice of God is heard and nobody else is on stage, lower the lights. If performed in the sanctuary, leave on any candelabra on either side of the Ark. This light and that of the *ner tamid* will produce a nice effect and will help to add variety, especially if there is no scenery.

OH GOD, MY GOD!

CHARACTERS:
- **Voice** — *This is the voice of God*
- **Angels** — *There are four of them representing: Peace, Love, Righteousness and Truth*
- **Adam**
- **Eve**
- **Moses**
- **Isaiah**
- **Members, Jerusalem Political Club**

(ALL THE LIGHTS IN THE SANCTUARY ARE TURNED OUT EXCEPT FOR THE EVERLASTING LIGHT AND THE *MENOROT* FLANKING THE ARK. A VOICE IS HEARD IN THE STILLNESS.)

Voice: (OFFSTAGE) There comes a time when even I need a vacation from all My worldly concerns. So many people and so many problems. Why, even when I created the earth I needed a day of rest. But lately it seems I am hearing so many complaints. So many people talking to Me all at one time. Parents complaining about their children... children complaining about their parents...So I decided to try and relax with a good book for a while. Well, of course, My book is the Book of Life. What memories came flooding into My mind as I leafed through the pages...After all, everyone who every lived is in it. Some pages brought so many tears... That's when the idea came to Me! Why not go to the people and tell you about My children and the problems I've encountered; maybe I could make you feel better. It's not easy being a parent either. Take it from one who knows. But it can also be the greatest joy. Sometimes just the decision to have a child takes a lot of thought and courage. I'll never forget that fateful day when I made the announcement to My angels.

SCENE I: Angels Meeting With God

(EACH ANGEL WEARS A DIFFERENT LARGE BADGE: PEACE, LOVE, RIGHTEOUSNESS AND TRUTH)

Angel 1: Why do you think the Lord has called this meeting today?

Angel 2: I don't know, but He seemed very preoccupied--as though something was troubling Him.

Angel 3: How could that be? Look at what He has created! A beautiful new world! Have you ever seen such trees and flowers! Such glorious colors!

Angel 4: And such beautiful crystal clear blue waters!

Angel 2: The Lord has created a masterpiece! He is the supreme artist.

Angel 1: Shhhh. I hear Him coming.

(SOUND OF THUNDER. THEN VOICE OF GOD IS HEARD.)

Voice: Thank you for coming, My good angels. I have something of the utmost importance to discuss with you.

All: Of course. What is it? We are here to help You in any way.

Voice: We have recently created a new world...

Angel 3: And it's so beautiful and peaceful...it's lovely, Lord.

Voice: But I'm not happy. There is something missing.

All: Missing? What? What is missing?

Angel 4: You have all kinds of vegetation and climates and animals. What would be missing?

Voice: I wish to create people!

All: People!! What's that?

Voice: Thinking, feeling and human types...after My own likeness—to carry out My will upon this new earth.

Angel 3: But if human beings can choose to do what they wish...if they can think, perhaps they will choose to do evil.

Angel 1: But then again, perhaps they will choose to do good, knowing that it will please the Lord. For this is what the Lord wants...

Angel 2: Lord of Hosts, forgive me, but I don't think it's such a good idea. It will spoil Your beautiful land.

Angel 4: I think that God knows best. If He wants to create human beings, He should!

All: (ARGUING) But they will spoil the earth. I don't think He should ...I think God knows what He is doing. But how will people know what the Lord requireth of them. God has His ways, don't worry. Don't you know that by now? It isn't safe. He shouldn't. Yes, He should. (THE ANGELS REPRESENTING THE FOLLOWING TRAITS WILL SAY RESPECTIVELY:
Love: Human beings will dispense acts of Love.
Truth: Human beings will be compounded of falsehood.
Righteousness: Human beings will perform righteous deeds.
Peace: Human beings will be full of strife.)

Voice: (THUNDER) My good angels, please let Me hear no more. Besides, all this arguing will do you no good. It's too late anyhow. I have already created the first human being! But do not fear, for the Lord knoweth the way of righteousness, but the way of the wicked shall perish. (DIM LIGHTS OUT)

Voice: So I went ahead. I created a man and then a woman. That was the easy part. It's raising them that's the problem. You know, I wanted them to be special, unlike any other animals I created, so I gave them the ability to think for themselves. I mean, we all want our children to be able to think for themselves, right? Our task in raising them is to work ourselves out of a job. So what happens? What's the first word out of their mouths? NO! And right off the bat, My children disobeyed Me. Remember Adam and Eve?

SCENE II: Adam and Eve

Eve: (RUNNING IN) Adam, look! Is this not a beautiful piece of fruit? So round, so firm and so delicious, too. You must try it.

Adam: Isn't that from the tree that the Lord, our God, said we must not eat of?

Eve: Oh, so what. He won't know. Besides, a friend of mine said the reason the Lord doesn't want us to have it is because it will make us too wise--that we'll be as wise as God Himself. So, go ahead. Eat it. It's O.K. (BLACKOUT)

Voice: So what do you do when your

children disobey. You have to punish them. She had to give birth with pain and he had to work for food by the sweat of his brow. And because I did not want them to eat from the tree of eternal life, I had to throw them out of the Garden of Eden altogether. Hopefully, it was to teach them a lesson. Then as I flipped through the pages of My book, I came across a very unusual person, Moses. But even he had moments of such stubbornness! Remember?

SCENE III: Moses Talking To God

Moses: (WALKING ALONG WITH HIS STAFF IN HIS HAND, PRODDING HIS IMAGINARY HERD) Go on now. Get along. Join the others. (SEES THE BURNING BUSH) What is that? The bush is on fire! But this is strange. It is not burning up. It remains whole. How can that be?

Voice: Moses! Moses!

Moses: Here I am. Who is there? I hear you, but I cannot see you.

Voice: Moses, take off your shoes. You are on holy ground. I am the Lord, your God, Moses. The God of your fathers, Abraham, Isaac and Jacob.

Moses: You've got to be kidding!

Voice: No, Moses. I'm telling the truth. Go on, take off your shoes.

(MOSES TAKES OFF HIS SHOES)

Moses: What do you want with me, God? I'm just a shepherd tending my flock.

Voice: Look, Moses. I have heard the cries of My people in their bondage in Egypt. They are your people, too. I have chosen you to go to Pharaoh and tell him to let My people go. And then you must go to My people and tell them that I have sent you to lead them out of Egypt.

Moses: (CHUCKLING) God, Listen. Do you really think Pharaoh is going to listen to me? He's going to let all his slaves go free just because I come before him and tell him to--just like that.

Voice: I know. I know. Pharaoh won't budge unless he is moved by force. Don't worry. I will cause horrible things to happen to him and to Egypt until he lets you all go. You can tell him that from Me.

Moses: And the Hebrew people, God. If I go to them and tell them that You and I have talked and You have sent me to help them, what's the first thing they're going to say? They're going to say, "If you and God are so friendly, what's His name?" Then what am I supposed to say?

Voice: Just say, *Ehyeh Asher Ehyeh* has sent you. I AM THAT I AM...

Ehyeh has sent you.

Moses: I don't think I can, God. I mean, they'll think I'm crazy. And certainly Pharaoh will laugh in my face...or have me killed. No, I'm sorry, but I don't think I can.

Voice: Moses, you have nothing to be afraid of. I am with you. And as for the people, I will give you some signs that will convince the people. Like the bush you just saw. Or better yet, throw down your rod...(MOSES TOSSES HIS STAFF ON THE FLOOR)

Moses: It has turned into a snake!

Voice: Now reach for it, Moses.

Moses: AHHHH! It is a rod again!

Voice: See! Now don't be so stubborn. Go and do what I ask you to do.

Moses: But I don't speak well. I can't go in there...

Voice: (VERY IMPATIENT) Then get Aaron, your brother, to help you. Let him do the talking, but you do the thinking, for I will be telling you what to say. Now go! Go! (BLACKOUT)

Voice: Oh, sometimes My patience is truly tested. But as you know, everything worked out. I suppose I shouldn't complain. On the whole I've had a lot of *"naches fun der kinder."*

There was Amos, Hosea, Jeremiah, Isaiah...Of course, it's not always easy to do what your parents say ...to do the right thing, especially when all your friends are doing the opposite. It takes a very special person. I'll never forget when Isaiah was invited to speak before the Political Club of Jerusalem. He knew full well what was going to happen, but he did it anyhow.

SCENE IV: Political Club Meeting

Lady I: Oh, I'm so excited. Imagine! Isaiah coming to speak to us!

Man I: He's one of the finest political speakers around. I thought of inviting him, you know. His visions have made him the most talked about person in the land!

Lady II: Well, it was a marvelous idea! He's supposed to be handsome, too. Do I look all right? I had this dress made just for today.

Lady III: And I bought this ring. It adds just the right touch, don't you think? One can't have too many, if you ask me. After all, I want to make the right impression.

Man II: I've never met anyone of his stature before. He's practically of royal blood...grew up in the palace. What's he talking about today, anyhow?

Man III: Who knows...who cares... he's so famous!

Lady IV: Oh, here he comes! Here he comes! Welcome, Isaiah. Welcome to the Political Club of Jerusalem. We boast of the finest families in Jerusalem.

Lady V: We're all just dying to hear you speak.

Lady I: Yes, this is quite a day for us.

Lady II: Now, we're all here, I'm going to introduce you. Ahem, ladies and gentlemen, if you'll be seated, we'll begin our program. Ahem, our distinguished guest has arrived...I know you're all just as anxious as I am to hear what he has to say, but first, let me tell you something about him. (SHE READS NOTES) Raised with all the possessions of the royal family, our guest could have become just another playboy, but did he? No! He chose to devote himself to the betterment of our country. He has sacrificed his own security and worldly goods in order to meet with, advise and counsel our leaders, trying to keep this country of ours secure and peaceful. Have we not all heard his warnings to the kingdom? Well, ladies and gentlemen of Jerusalem, we are here today to listen to the wise counsel of our honored speaker...I am happy to present: Isaiah.

Isaiah: Sons and daughters of Jerusalem, I am happy that you have invited me here today.

Voice: Remember, Isaiah, what you have to do.

Isaiah: I come not to tell you what you want to hear, but what you must hear. You think you are safe from conquest, that the Lord does not see your wicked ways. Well, let me tell you, the Lord sees all, and you are going to bring disaster upon all our heads because all you care about are material things and have no morals. You have sunk to a new low!

All: (GASPING)

Isaiah: Because the daughters of Zion are haughty and walk with outstretched necks and wanton eyes, instead of sweet perfumery--there shall be rottenness. Instead of girdle--a rope. Instead of permanent waves--baldness. Instead of a robe--a girding of sackcloth. Instead of beauty--branding.

All: Has he lost his senses! I will not listen to such vile talk! How dare he! He has gone mad! I'll tell the King, he'll see to him! Get him out of here. I've never been so humiliated...so outraged! Get out! Get out! (THEY CHASE HIM OUT AND AS THEY DO SO, THE LIGHTS SLOWLY GO OUT LEAVING THE ROOM DARK AS IT WAS IN THE BEGINNING)

Voice: No, it's not easy for a parent to sit back and suffer at the hands of wickedness. And it isn't easy to do what's right all the time. But Isaiah knew what he had to do, because he spoke for Me. And just as I have pointed the way for Isaiah to see the right, your parents point the way for you, for they are My messengers on earth. That is why I have given you the commandment, "Honor Thy Father and Thy Mother," for the ways of the world are mysterious and sometimes when they say no to you, they are saying yes to Me.

(BLACKOUT)

And Brings Us to This Season

Grades 7-12

PRODUCTION NOTES

The only scenery necessary for this play is a small table covered with a cloth. The cloth can be changed for one of white lace or other dressy fabric when it is time to set the table for dinner. No one should be seated with his or her back to the audience; the actors will have to "cheat" a little for the table to accommodate five people.

The scene at the synagogue should be entered from a different access than the house scene to let the audience know that the action takes place somewhere else. Also, play the entire synagogue scene on a different area of the stage if this is possible.

AND BRINGS US TO THIS SEASON: A THANKSGIVING PLAY

CHARACTERS:

    Daughter   Grandson

    Grandfather   Granddaughter

    Son-in-Law   Rabbi

    Men and Women of the Synagogue Committee

SCENE I: At the Kitchen Table

(GRANDPA IS POURING HIMSELF A GLASS OF TEA. HE FORGETS TO PUT IN THE SPOON. THE GLASS GETS TOO HOT AND HE DROPS AND SPILLS THE TEA AND THE TEAPOT, BREAKING THE TEAPOT. AS THIS HAPPENS, HIS DAUGHTER ENTERS. SHE BECOMES ANGRY AND SAYS:)

Daughter: Oh, no! My best teapot! It was an antique. I'll never be able to replace it. Honestly, Dad, can't you be more careful? If you would use a cup for your tea instead of a glass, this wouldn't happen. I've asked you a million times...

Grandfather: I'm sorry--I guess I forgot to put in the spoon. It got too hot. Here, I'll clean it up, don't worry.

Daughter: Never mind, I'll clean it up. Just do me a favor and stay out of the kitchen. Every time you come in here, you make more work for me. If you want something, just ask for it.

Grandfather: All right, all right--I can see I'm just in the way around here. But you don't have to treat me like a child--after all, I still am your father. I knew this would never work--I suppose it's time for me to move out.

Daughter: Oh, Dad, don't be silly. Where would you go? Besides, we want you here. Only please be careful with my things--O.K.?
(DAUGHTER EXITS. GRANDFATHER SHRUGS HIS SHOULDERS, SHAKES HIS HEAD AND GOES OFF, TOO.)

SCENE II: Outside the Synagogue

(DAUGHTER AND TWO OTHER PEOPLE ENTER AS THOUGH THEY HAVE JUST COME FROM A MEETING AT THE SYNAGOGUE. CHARACTERS WEAR COATS TO SUGGEST AN OUTSIDE SCENE.)

Man I: Well, that was a nice short meeting for a change.

Man II: Yeah, but we really got a lot accomplished. Looks like the synagogue is going to have a really good schedule of programs this year. Lots of variety--there should be something for everyone.

Daughter: Yes, and I've got to get busy right away. I'm in charge of the Chanukah program and I've got to find a committee to help. I don't know how I'll get it all done--I've got so much else going on right now.

Man I: Oh, you'll manage, you always do. This synagogue couldn't function without you. Are you feeling all right? It's not like you to let things like this upset you.

Daughter: Oh, I'm all right. I guess I'm just a little edgy. I lost my temper with my father today and I'm feeling guilty about it. But honestly, he just aggravates me sometimes. It's not easy having him under foot all the time. You don't know how lucky you are not having a parent living with you.

Man II: Oh, I don't know about that. My father was a fantastic person. I'd give anything to have him back again. I really miss him, especially at holiday time.

Rabbi: (ENTERS) Well, what are you all still doing here? I thought the meeting ended a while ago. Can't tear yourself away, huh?

Daughter: Oh, hi Rabbi. We were just discussing the problems of having a third generation living in the same house. It's not easy, you know.

Rabbi: So, who promised you that everything would be easy? You know, too often we don't appreciate what we have until we don't have it anymore. It might be an old saying, but it's true.

Man II: Right you are, Rabbi.

Rabbi: I'll tell you, sometimes it's not easy just having two generations in the house. Parents are unhappy with their kids--kids get impatient with their parents. They can't wait to grow up and move out. What was it I read the other day in the newspaper...Oh, yes... Just about the time our children finally stop doing and saying things that embarrass us in public, we begin doing and saying things that embarrass them. Well, good night everyone.

All: Goodnight, Rabbi. Goodnight. See you soon. (ALL SAY GOODNIGHT TO EACH OTHER AND EXIT)

SCENE III: In the Kitchen

Grandson: Hey, Gramps, how do you spell "governor?"

Grandfather: Sound it out--govern-or ...g-o-v-e-r-n-o-r. What are you writing about?

Grandson: Oh, every November we have to write a theme about Thanksgiving. I'm writing about Governor Bradford. Did you know that he modeled Thanksgiving after Sukkot?

Grandfather: Of course, he not only modeled it after Sukkot, but he actually quoted the Hebrew text. Did you know that Governor Bradford knew how to read Hebrew?

Grandson: No, I didn't. How did you know?

Grandfather: Oh, I read and study. Just because I'm not in school anymore doesn't mean my education stops.

Grandson: Gee, thanks, Gramps. That'll be great to put in my theme.

Granddaughter: Excuse me, Gramps. Mom asked me to set the table for dinner and I'm really jammed up. I've got a ton of reading to do for English Lit.

Grandfather: So, let me help you. I've got nothing important to do. (HELPS SET THE TABLE AS THE CONVERSATION GOES ON) So tell me, what are you reading?

Granddaughter: Well, we were given a whole list of quotations and we have to look up the author and then tell where each came from and explain its meaning. Right now I'm on the quotation that's on the Statue of Liberty.

Grandfather: Oh you mean, "Give me your tired, your poor..."

Granddaughter: Yes, that's the one. How do you know it?

Grandfather: Anyone who came to this country as an immigrant should know that. It's by Emma Lazarus, a very great poetess. Did you know she was Jewish?

Granddaughter: No, I didn't. How did you know? Gosh, you know so many things. Wait, I'm going to get my book. Maybe you could help me with some of the other quotations, too. (SHE EXITS)

Grandson: Uhmmm. Smell that turkey. I'm starving.

Grandfather: And when aren't you starving? I don't know where you put all the food you eat.

Grandson: It's too bad Aunt Sue and Uncle Mike and the kids couldn't be here. It's the first Thanksgiving that we're not all together.

Grandfather: Yes, it'll be a quiet one, but at least they're off enjoying themselves, and we're all together and healthy, thank God.

Daughter: Dinner's ready! Let's all sit down. (EVERYONE COMES IN AND SITS DOWN AT THE TABLE)

Son-in-Law: First of all, I think we should start this meal off with a *Shehecheyanu*, to be grateful that we are all together at this Thanksgiving time.

All: (RECITE *SHEHECHEYANU)*

Grandfather: You're right, son. Really, everyday is a day of thanksgiving just as long as we can all be together.

Son-in-Law: That's right, Pop. We really take so many things for granted. Oh, I don't mean just material things like food or clothing—but just waking up every morning, feeling good, being part of a family that loves you and that you can share things with.

Daughter: You know, I feel so guilty for not appreciating the really important things. Like you, Pop. I am so ashamed of the way I've been treating you. You have given me so much—your time, your love, the benefit of your experience—and I've been so short-tempered in return.

Son-in-Law: I think we all are at times. We get so involved with ourselves, we forget to, how does that song go, "stop and smell the roses"—

Granddaughter: Hey, Dad, how do you know that?

Daughter: I guess we really do need holidays to remind us.

Grandfather: Remind us?

Daughter: Yes, remind us that we're never too old to learn, or to be taken over our father's knee for a good spanking when we need it. (ALL LAUGH) Dad, I'm very thankful for you and very glad that you're here.

Grandson: Me, too. You should see how he helps me with my homework.

Granddaughter: And me, too!

Father: Well, let's all lift our glasses in a toast of thanksgiving—to Grandpa.

All: TO GRANDPA! *L' Chaim*!!

The Sacrifice

Grades 5-8

PRODUCTION NOTES

This play is best performed on a stage utilizing a curtain, stage lighting and a follow spot. Scenery can be as elaborate as desired. The set can be made in three sections and lighting used to black out the sections not being used. Place a raised platform on stage right backed by a couple of folding screens covered with brown paper. On the paper a window can be drawn of the sort that might be found in a hut. Paint some jars on the sill. Hang wicker baskets on the walls and place others on the floor.

Use a scrim at center stage. This is a large wooden frame over which is stretched a very thin piece of material. When a spotlight is shone from behind, it produces a shadow effect. The fight scene can be done in the shadows with stirring music playing on tape and timed for the length of the scene. The scene in the enemy camp can take place on stage left in front of a makeshift tent. Create Lev's torch by tying strips of red and yellow gel over a flashlight.

THE SACRIFICE

CHARACTERS:

Teacher	– Old and kind
Lev	– A headstrong and brave young boy
Mother	– Lev's mother, a widow
Yehudit	– Her friend
Rifka	– Yehudit's daughter, a friend of Lev
Eliezer	– Another boy

Greek/Syrian Guards

School Children and Friends of the Mother

SCENE I: In the School

(OPENS WITH THE ACTORS REPRESENTING SCHOOL CHILDREN SITTING IN THE FRONT ROW WITH THE AUDIENCE. THE OLD TEACHER IS STANDING BEFORE THEM, FACING THE AUDIENCE ON A RISER. THE CURTAINS ARE CLOSED. THE TEACHER IS IN A SPOTLIGHT. THE WHOLE ATMOSPHERE IS ONE OF MOURNING.)

Teacher: My children, we have spent a lot of time together in this little room. Some of you have studied hard and learned your lessons well ...Others...well...some of you dream of chasing butterflies instead, but you have all been good children.

Child I: What's wrong? Why do you speak as if in the past?

Child II: (TO ANOTHER) What's wrong with the teacher today?

Teacher: Today is our last time together. Aniochus puts our lives in danger. He will not allow any more teaching of tradition. How can we pass on to you, our children, the greatness and the wonder of our people?

Child III: Where will we go to study?

Teacher: (SHAKING HIS HEAD) I don't know. Many families are already fleeing from our town and going into the hills to escape from the Greek soldiers.

Child IV: They killed my friend last week. They told him to bow down to their idol, and when he said no, they killed him and laughed.

Teacher: What will become of us...I don't know. We must all do what we think is best. Use our conscience to guide us. Do what we know in our hearts is the right thing to do.

Lev: I know what I'm going to do... I'm going to join the Maccabees! I'm going to fight! No one is going to come into my country and threaten me without a fight!

All: (LAUGHING) Lev, don't be silly ...you're only 15...and with a bad leg, too...a lot of good you'll be

...Some soldier! Dream on, Lev!

Teacher: A fine sentiment...but, I don't know, we have to be realistic. What kind of chance do we have against a mighty Syrian army?

Child V: There are so many soldiers everywhere...my mother has become afraid even to go to the marketplace.

Child VI: My father thinks we should fight. He has been going to meetings at night. If I were older, I would fight, too.

Lev: Well, I'm going to! You'll see ...You can laugh if you want, but you'll see. I'm going with Judah --the Maccabee!

Teacher: Goodbye, my children, go and play and try to enjoy life, but do not forget all you have learned here.

SCENE II: In the House

(THE CURTAIN OPENS AS THE CHILDREN WALK UP ONTO THE STAGE. THEY REMAIN IN A FROZEN POSITION AS IF PLAYING. LEV WALKS INTO HIS HOUSE. THE SUGGESTION OF AN INTERIOR OF A MODEST ROOM IS STAGE RIGHT. HIS MOTHER IS ALREADY THERE. AS THE PLAYING OF THE CHILDREN DIES DOWN, THE SPOTLIGHT COMES UP ON THE SCENE IN THE HOUSE AS THOUGH IN THE MIDDLE OF A CONVERSATION.)

Mother: Lev, you are too young. You

mustn't think of such things. And your leg...

Lev: My leg is fine...look...I am getting better all the time. I don't even need this old thing anymore, really. (HE TOSSES THE WALKING STICK AWAY)

Mother: Oh, if only your father were alive. If only the Lord had spared him from the accident the way He saw fit to spare you. Blessed be His name. Oh, but I mustn't question His ways. Thank God, you're with me. I can't bear to think of you in danger...

Lev: Listen to me, Mother...we are all in danger. Right now! Right here! You are in danger! I am in danger! No one is safe and there is no one to prevent these vicious soldiers from storming into our house and killing us now! (KNOCK ON THE DOOR IS HEARD)

Mother: (STARTLED) Who can that be?

Lev: I will see. Who is there?

Yehudit: It is I, Yehudit, and my daughter, Rifka. May we come in?

Mother: Of course...of course. Excuse us, but you can't be too careful these days.

Yehudit: You are right. I just stopped by to see if there is anything you need. My husband is taking me to the marketplace. I thought I would save you a trip.

Mother: How nice of you. Come sit and talk for a minute.

Rifka: (TO LEV) Are you really going to join Judah, Lev? I heard what you said in school today.

Lev: I meant what I said, Rifka. I will not lie down and have my nose rubbed in the dirt! All around us people are being murdered for no reason!

Rifka: But, Lev, what can you do? You're only a boy...and one person! There are hundreds of guards around us. Just look outside; they are all over the street. (THEY MOVE TO THE EDGE OF THE HOUSE AND PEER OUT AS THE LIGHT FADES ON THEM AND COMES UP ON THE STREET)

SCENE III: In the Street

Guard I: How much longer do you think we'll have to stay in this place?

Guard II: No telling, but it's not so bad. We get plenty of food and plenty of sport--watch this... Hey, you! (TO A BOY IN THE STREET)

Boy I: (FRIGHTENED) Who, me?

Guard II: Yes, you! Bow down to the king of the gods. Bow to Zeus!

Eliezer: We bend our knees only to one God--to Adonai.

Guard I: Run him through! See then

how he'll bow! (LAUGHS)

Boy II: Bow, Eliezer, don't be stupid. It doesn't matter...Save yourself! (PUSHES HIM DOWN)

Guard II: Ha, Ha! Listen to your friend, Eliezer! He uses his head. And you'd better use yours, too—unless you want to see it on top of this! (HOLDS UP SWORD)

Guard III: A strong boy like you should be training in our gymnasiums, participating in our arenas, building up your body, not wasting your time filling your head full of worthless nonsense.

Guard II: Come, let us see what we can find to eat. (TO ELIEZER) You'll do well to learn the ways of the Greeks. (EXITS)

Eliezer: I spit on you and your idols!

Boy III: Eliezer, be careful. You'll get us all killed.

Eliezer: Lev was right. We can not wait here and be humiliated—or worse—slaughtered! We should all join the armies of Judah.

Lev: (ENTERING) Eliezer, I saw what happened. You are very brave.

Eliezer: Lev, I heard what you said in school today. Are you really going to join the Maccabees?

Lev: I want to, but...

Rifka: He better not. He'll be killed—he's only a boy. What would your mother say?

Lev: I'm 15. I don't have to ask my mother. I'll go if I want to...

Girl I: Well, are you going to or have you changed your mind?

Girl II: Maybe he's decided it's too dangerous for him after all...

Eliezer: Be quiet! Lev, do you really think you would be of help?

Lev: I don't know, but I've got to try. All I know is that up there in the mountains are gathered the strength and courage of my people. They will not lie down like lambs... they choose to fight like lions! Fight for freedom.

Eliezer: Yes, I heard Judah when he came to gather men here in the marketplace..."*Mi Ladonai Elai,*" he said..."Whoever is for the Lord, follow me!"

Lev: And so I must follow, too.

Rifka: Be careful, Eliezer. The Syrian camp lies between here and Judah's army.

Boy: What if they catch you?

Lev: I'll be all right.

Eliezer: Goodbye, Lev. Good luck.

Girl III: Go with God, Lev.

Lev: (TO RIFKA) Tell my mother... tell my mother that I had no choice...this is something I have to do. (BLACKOUT)

SCENE IV: Behind the Scrim

(MUSIC UP...LIGHT COMES UP BEHIND THE SCRIM...WE SEE THE SHADOW OF LEV CREEPING STEALTHILY ACROSS THE STAGE BEHIND THE SCRIM...ALL OF A SUDDEN SHADOWS OF SOLDIERS APPEAR... THE MUSIC CRESCENDOES...A STRUGGLE IS SEEN...THE BOY FALLS...MUSIC OUT)

SCENE V: The Enemy Camp

Guard: (LIGHTS COME UP ON LEV TIED UP...GUARDS STANDING BY. HEAD GUARD COMES OUT.) Well, boy. You're lucky you're not dead. But we can use a healthy young boy like you. We've got a lot of jobs around here that need doing...polishing swords, cooking, cleaning tents...

Soldier: Sir, all the plans are set. We will be ready for them.

Lev: Ready for whom?

Guard: It may interest you to know that your friend, Judah, plans to attack our camp tonight, but we found out...our spies do their work well.

Soldier: And we will be ready for them...we have a few surprises of our own! Ha, Ha.

Guard: Here, you can begin by polishing this...and I wouldn't try to run away. There are guards all around you. (EXITS)

Lev: (ALONE...OUT LOUD TO HIMSELF) I must find a way to warn Judah of the trap, but how? There is no way out of here for me. And I know if I yell or raise an alarm, the Syrians will kill me...(THINKING TO HIMSELF) Mother, I'm sorry ...I'm sorry.

SCENE VI: In the House

Mother: (LIGHTS UP ON INSIDE OF HOUSE. MOTHER AND SEVERAL OF HER FRIENDS SEEN, WEEPING.) And Rifka came to tell me that Lev has gone to join Judah.

Friend I: Be brave, Yehudit; your son is brave and for his sake you must be, too.

Friend II: He has placed the safety and freedom of his people before that of his own. All through our history there have been men and women who have done this...and we honor them and praise them. That is why we have survived until now. Lev is a hero, Yehudit. (BLACKOUT)

SCENE VII: The Enemy Camp

(VERY DIM LIGHT, PRACTICALLY DARK ...ONLY SHADOWS ARE SEEN)

Guard: (STAGE WHISPER) Is everything set?

Soldier: Yes. All is ready. Where is the boy?

Guard: He's in the cook's tent keeping the flame alive so that there will be warm food for us after the battle has been won.

Guard: Too bad for Judah. What do his people call him? The Maccabee? The Hammer! Well, we'll see who will deliver the fatal blow this time, Hammer...Ha, Ha...

(TAPED VOICES OF JUDAH'S CAMP ARE HEARD FROM THE BACK OF THE HOUSE. MUSIC, PLAYED UNDER THE VOICES, APPROACHES SLOWLY AND BECOMES LOUDER AS IT MOVES THROUGH THE DARK HOUSE, GETTING CLOSER TO THE STAGE AS THOUGH AN ARMY WERE QUIETLY ADVANCING.)

Soldier: Quiet! I hear something!

Guard: Everyone in position. (WHISPERING)

Soldier: Here they come. Here they come. Ready now...

(ALL OF A SUDDEN LEV DASHES ON THE STAGE WITH A LIGHTED TORCH AND SHOUTS)

Lev: Judah, it's a trap! Go back! Go back! They know you are coming. Go back!

Guard: Silence that boy! Quick! (LOT OF BACKGROUND NOISE. LEV IS FELLED. THE LIGHTS ARE EXTINGUISHED, THEN SILENCE. STAGE GOES BLACK.)

SCENE VIII: The School

Teacher: (PIN SPOT UP ON OLD TEACHER. THE CHILDREN ARE SEATED IN A SEMICIRCLE IN FRONT OF HIM, THEIR BACKS TO THE AUDIENCE.) And so, my children...once again we can gather to learn of our history, to speak and study tradition. And we will celebrate this victory for our freedom forever...And every year when we light our *chanukiah* to remember God's miracles, let us not forget that this flame of freedom that we display so proudly in our windows is also a memorial candle ...a memorial to all who have died so that we might live...And let us all say together the prayer of thanks to God that we have reached this season of joy and can celebrate it together.
(MOTIONS TO THE AUDIENCE TO JOIN IN. ALL SAY *SHEHECHEYANU*)

(BLACKOUT)

God's Wide Spaces

Grades 7-12

PRODUCTION NOTES

The stage should be made to look like the sparse and bare kitchen of a very poor *kibbutz* in 1922. Hang on the back curtain or wall a simple brown paper backdrop with a painted window and sill with flowerpot, and with various pots and pans hanging nearby. A stove can be improvised from crates or boxes so that it can actually be functional on the surface and can hold a kettle. There is a long table with an odd assortment of chairs set around it. The table is covered with a white sheet and a small vase of greenery is in the middle. An unmatched set of mugs are placed around for the correct number of people and an odd assortment of silverware. A *challah* is on the table. Plates of food will be handed from the stove during the action of the play. The whole atmosphere should suggest the most meager surroundings.

The scene depicted here is fictional, as are all the characters except Golda. The place, however, Kibbutz Merhavia in the Emek Valley, is an actual place and all the information about the lifestyle there is factual. IT IS EXTREMELY IMPORTANT FOR THE DRAMATIC EFFECT OF THE ENDING NOT TO REVEAL THE IDENTITY OF GOLDA TO THE AUDIENCE IN ANY WAY PRIOR TO THE ENDING OF THE PLAY.

GOD'S WIDE SPACES

CHARACTERS:

    Golda   Morris

    Sarah   Rachel

    Esther   Leah

    Lev   Narrator

    Gordon

(THE PLAY OPENS WITH THE CLANGING OF A LOUD BELL, LIKE A COW BELL. TWO WOMEN ARE ALREADY ON STAGE PREPARING DINNER. ONE IS AT THE STOVE STIRRING SOMETHING IN A LARGE KETTLE. THE OTHER IS PLACING A VASE OF GREENS IN THE CENTER OF THE TABLE.)

Golda: Here, you can fill the cups while I stir this. (SHE HANDS SARAH A LARGE JUG) Everyone should be coming in soon.

Sarah: (SHE WALKS AROUND THE TABLE POURING FROM THE JUG INTO EACH ONE OF THE MUGS) Another Shabbat! Somehow we've gotten through another whole week! How I hate the winter. So much rain...every day, rain! And mud! Everything I own is so caked with mud, I can't get anything clean anymore!

Golda: (WALKING TO HER) Sarah, Sarah. What's the matter? We are all in this together. It's not easy for any of us. At least we're not covered with flies and mosquitoes like in the summer, right?

Sarah: At least you are married. You have Morris. You have someone who cares about you! Here I am with nothing and nobody! And what for?

Golda: Sarah...you know what for. Do I have to tell you? You came here to Merhavia for the same reason we did. We are building for the future. And it's not true that you have nobody. If you lived in the city alone in a cramped apartment--then you would have nobody! But here, here--on our *kibbutz*, you have all of us! We are all your family. We care about you!

Sarah: I'm sorry--I don't know what got into me. I just...

(SHE IS INTERRUPTED BY SEVERAL PEOPLE ENTERING TALKING AND LAUGHING, INCLUDING MORRIS, GORDON, ESTHER AND LEV, WHO PLACES HIS SHOVEL AGAINST THE WALL. EVERYONE IS DRESSED IN VERY MODEST, BUT OBVIOUSLY CLEAN, FRESH CLOTHING FOR SHABBAT. THE MEN HAVE THEIR SHIRTSLEEVES ROLLED UP OR WEAR SHORT SLEEVES WITH SWEATERS SINCE IT IS THE WINTER SEASON. THE WOMEN WEAR DRESSES SUGGESTING THE EARLY 20's. THEY ALSO WEAR EITHER A RAINCOAT OR HEAVY SWEATER AND PERHAPS A KERCHIEF ON THEIR HEADS.)

Lev: And so I think we should put our

money into more chickens. In fact, I have heard of a special agricultural school to study poultry breeding and I think we should elect one of us to go there. We should go about this in a scientific way if we are looking to make a profit.

Morris: (HE CROSSES OVER TO GOLDA AS HE SPEAKS AND INTERRUPTS HIMSELF WITH A KISS ON GOLDA'S CHEEK) We have enough chickens for now. Good Shabbos. How about some decent plumbing!

Gordon: That's right! This is 1922! There are so many conveniences we could buy with the money we are making.

Morris: That's right! We are harvesting a good almond crop and selling our milk to Haifa!

Sarah: I would like to buy a new dress! I am sick of wearing the same thing every day...and one old *shmata* for Shabbat!

Golda: Calm down, everyone! Calm down. Sit. Dinner is ready. The sun has gone down. Let's have a peaceful Shabbat. No business talk right now. Sarah, why don't you light the candles?

Sarah: (SHE SHAKES HER HEAD) Not tonight.

Golda: Esther? (OFFERING HER THE MATCHES)

Esther: Yes, certainly. (SHE LIGHTS

THE CANDLES AND RECITES THE BLESSING OVER THEM)

Lev: And now the wine. (HE RAISES HIS MUG AND EVERYONE ELSE DOES THE SAME. HE RECITES THE *KIDDUSH*. EVERYONE SAYS "AMEN."

Gordon: Sarah, the *challah* looks delicious. You are surely the best *challah* baker for miles around.

Morris: Of course, there is no one else *but* us for miles around. (THEY ALL LAUGH AND EVENTUALLY SARAH JOINS IN)

Rachel: (RUNNING IN BREATHLESSLY) Everyone! Everyone! Look who is here! (SHE GRABS A SHY, YOUNG GIRL BY THE ARM AND PULLS HER INTO THE ROOM, SHOVING HER FORWARD) Here is my sister, Leah, from Lithuania. She has come to live with us here at Merhavia. Everyone, meet Leah!

All: (NODDING, SMILING, WAVING) Welcome! Welcome to Merhavia. Welcome to our oasis in the midst of the Emek Valley.

Golda: Please join us, Leah. You're just in time for Shabbat dinner.

Leah: (SMILES SHYLY AND SITS AT A PLACE POINTED OUT FOR HER AT THE TABLE) *Todah Rabah*.

Gordon: Ah, already she speaks Hebrew! Here, let me get you some food. (HE RISES AND CROSSES TO THE STOVE, SPOONING FOOD ONTO

A DISH. WHILE HE IS GONE, LEV MOVES OVER, SITS BY LEAH AND BEGINS TO SPEAK TO HER. GORDON RETURNS EXPECTING TO SIT THERE. HE GIVES LEV A DIRTY LOOK AS HE HANDS LEAH HER PLATE. HE REMAINS STANDING BEHIND THEM A FEW SECONDS, FINALLY RESIGNING HIMSELF TO TAKING ANOTHER SEAT.)

Lev: (APOLOGETICALLY) We don't have too much to offer yet.

Sarah: We have plenty of mud.

Lev: (IGNORING THAT REMARK) Chicken is for Shabbat only. The rest of the week we eat the vegetables that we grow here and something called *chumis*, which is made out of chick peas.

Sarah: I call it mush. But you'll learn to pretend just like the rest of us. One night it's caviar; the next, filet mignon! (SHE SAYS THIS SARCASTICALLY)

Golda: Come! Let's not scare Leah. After all, she just got here and doesn't know our sense of humor just yet. (TO LEAH) It's really not so bad. The winter gets us down sometimes. So much rain. But soon it will be Tu B'Shvat! The beginning of spring. The almond trees will blossom and the entire Emek Valley will be covered with a carpet of the most beautiful wild flowers that I have ever seen! I'll never forget my first spring here. I thought it was the most lovely sight in the whole world! And then...

Morris: And then the real work begins! Planting!

Golda: Oh, but the trees! How we need them!

Esther: You should see the harvest we get from our almond trees. A lot of the money we make here on our *kibbutz* comes from that. You'll wind up picking almonds, too. Here everyone winds up doing just about everything.

Rachel: Although sometimes we women get stuck in the kitchen more than we'd like. We have to fight for our rights even here. We want to be out working in the fields just like the men! You can't imagine the feeling of kneeling down in that sandy, rocky soil and watering a little sapling and knowing that someday it is going to be a giant tree and that you did it with your own hands!

Leah: That's what you've said in your letters. That's why I'm here. I want to know that feeling, too.

Sarah: It's a wonder that anything grows. It's nothing but rock out there.

Rachel: That's just my point! We are making miracles here every day!

Golda: You know the road you drove down coming here? Did you see all those trees?

Morris: You could hardly call them trees yet.

Golda: (SHE GOES RIGHT ON AS IF HE HADN'T SPOKEN) We planted them! Oh, will I ever forget the row upon row of holes we dug between the rocks and how we carefully planted each little sapling.

Lev: And even as we planted, we wondered if they would ever grow. But you saw! They're alive and well!

Gordon: They're still small, but they are growing--and someday they will be a forest! A forest! And we will have done it!

Leah: What kind of trees are they?

Esther: Olive trees and almond trees for harvesting. We can sell the crops to nearby cities and villages.

Morris: But there are also some trees that don't bear any fruit.

Sarah: But all the trees are necessary to keep the soil from being blown and washed away. You wouldn't have believed this place when the first settlers came here in 1911. A wasteland! If it wasn't rocks, it was swamp. It all had to be drained and filled and cultivated...

Esther: But what we've managed to do! Maybe you couldn't see it--it gets dark early in the winter, but we have a large vegetable garden

...and cows and chickens and orchards...

Golda: You are a good omen, Leah! All of a sudden there is renewed spirit. That's what talking of spring does. It's time for a song! Lead us in singing, Lev. We need to sing of Shabbat and of Tu B'Shvat and of spring.

Lev: (GETTING UP QUICKLY FROM HIS CHAIR) What should we sing? How about...(HE BEGINS TO HUM, THEN SING "SHABBAT SHALOM." ALL THE REST JOIN IN.)

Rachel: Oh, Lev, it's almost Tu B'Shvat. Play *"Atzey Zetim Omdim."* (THEY ALL BEGIN TO SING. A FEW GET UP AND FORM A SEMICIRCLE. THEY LINK ARMS AND DANCE A HORA. AS THE SINGING DIES DOWN, ALL BEGIN TO LAUGH AND OBVIOUSLY OUT OF BREATH, FLOP DOWN ON CHAIRS. AS THEY FINISH, GORDON BRINGS OVER A PLATE OF COOKIES AND PASSES THEM AROUND.)

Gordon: Here! Cookies! (THEY ALL TAKE ONE, AD-LIBBING AS THEY DO ABOUT HOW GOOD THE COOKIES ARE OR HOW TIRED THEY ARE)

Sarah: I never thought the highlight of my week would be a cookie!

Rachel: (TO LEAH) We only have cookies on Shabbat. We have to save the flour and sugar. It's a special treat.

Morris: Well, I'm going to turn in.

Shabbat or no Shabbat, the cows have to be milked in the morning and I have to be up at four o'clock. Goodnight, everyone.

Lev: I've got some reading to do. I'll say goodnight, too.

Gordon: Me, too.

Golda: I'll be along after I straighten up, Morris. (HE NODS AND THE THREE MEN LEAVE)

Leah: Oh, I'll help you. It'll make me feel like I belong here.

Golda: That's wonderful, Leah. Sarah, you go to bed. Maybe you're coming down with something.

Sarah: (SHE NODS) Thanks, Leah. Goodnight. Are you coming to the room, Esther? Rachel?

Esther: Yes. (SHE CROSSES TO LEAH AND TAKES HER HANDS) We are so happy to have you here with us. Don't be afraid. We are all your family and will be here to help you in any way we can. (SHE TURNS TO GO OUT)

Rachel: Leah, I'll take your suitcases to our room.

Leah: Thanks, Rachel. (RACHEL AND ESTHER EXIT, LEAVING LEAH AND GOLDA ALONE ON THE STAGE)

Leah: (BEGINS CLEARING THE TABLE) I can't believe I am finally here. *Eretz Yisrael!* I have dreamed of coming here ever since Rachel left home, but my parents wouldn't let me come then. I was only 15. But now I am 18 and my parents knew that this was my destiny, too. Oh, listen to me talk so much. I'm sorry.

Golda: Don't be sorry. It's refreshing. Sometimes the work and the weather and the sickness here...it gets us down, but we, too, have a destiny. This country has a destiny and no little job is unimportant. We are going to make this land bloom again!

Leah: Yes, that's how Rachel feels, too. And me, too! I can't wait to begin working here.

Golda: Don't worry. There's plenty of that. The almond trees will begin to bloom shortly. That's the first sign of spring. Next week is Tu B'Shvat--the rains will just about have ended and the planting will begin. And each little sapling that we stick in the ground is a symbol of our belief that they and this country will grow and flourish. I only hope I'll live to see the forests of my labors. But this I know. There is nowhere on earth that I'd rather be than right here at Merhavia. Do you know what that means? Merhavia?

Leah: No, I don't.

Golda: It means "God's Wide Spaces." And that's what it was. But the wide spaces are being filled in with trees and houses and gardens ...the signs of life! So in spite of the heat and the flies in the summer and the mud and the rain in the winter...the outhouses and the meager food...we'll go on! We're just like those trees we plant. Some people think we'll never make it. "How can anything grow in sand and rock?" they say. But we'll show them. We may be little saplings now, but give us time. One day we'll be a forest! And you'll be part of it! (BY THIS TIME THEY HAVE CLEARED AWAY ALL THE DISHES AND A SEMBLANCE OF ORDER IS IN THE ROOM) And now, dear Leah, we must say goodnight, too.

Leah: (HUGGING HER) Oh, thank you. Thank you so much! Rachel showed me where our room was before we came into dinner. I'll find my way all right. (SHE BEGINS TO GO OUT, THEN STOPS AND TURNS AROUND) I feel so silly. I don't even know your name.

Golda: (SHE HAS TURNED UPSTAGE TO THE STOVE WHEN LEAH BEGAN TO GO OUT AND NOW SLOWLY TURNS AROUND TO FACE HER) It's Golda. Golda Meirson.

(AN OFFSTAGE VOICE IS AMPLIFIED AND HEARD AS GOLDA BUSIES HERSELF CLEARING THE REST OF THE TABLE, PERHAPS BRUSHING CRUMBS, BUT KEEPING HERSELF BUSY, TIMING HERSELF TO BE ABLE TO TAKE THE

WHITE SHEET OFF THE TABLE AND HOLD IT UP CENTER STAGE SO THAT BY THE TIME HER NAME, GOLDA MEIR, IS SAID, A SLIDE OF GOLDA MEIR CAN BE SHOWN AGAINST THE CLOTH AND HELD UNTIL THE END OF THE SPEECH. A GRADUALLY SWELLING RENDITION OF *"HATIKVAH"* CAN BE PLAYED UNDER THE NARRATION AND SHOULD BE TIMED TO END JUST AFTER THE LAST WORDS, AT WHICH TIME THERE SHOULD BE A BLACKOUT)

Narrator: Merhavia grew to become a big bustling settlement with a regional high school, industry, agriculture and comfortable, modern living facilities for all its members. And Golda Meir, as she became known, left to become involved in the making of a State. Intelligent, strong willed, hardworking and filled with a passion to rebuild the land, she became a diplomat and world traveler on behalf of Israel --Ambassador to Russia, Minister of Labor, and--in 1969--Prime Minister of the State of Israel! Like the many trees she planted, her beginnings in Palestine were fragile and shaky, but she took root, grew and blossomed just as the land she loved so well. For all you did-- *Todah*, Golda!

(BLACKOUT)

Purimspiel

Grades 5-12

PRODUCTION NOTES

This play can be performed on floor level with the audience seated in a semicircle around the stage area or, preferably, on a proscenium stage. The scenery should be very sketchy. Large, gaily painted cutouts can be used. Modern clothing can be adapted as necessary. For instance, the simpleton can wear jeans rolled up to just below the knee with loud striped knee socks and colorful suspenders. A shirt with a crazy design and a floppy hat would finish off this costume. The remainder of the costumes can be done either in modern dress or in traditional costumes. For instance, the storyteller might wear white pants and a brightly colored T-shirt lettered to read "STORYTELLER" across the front. The helpers might wear running shorts over matching tights and different colored T-shirts lettered to read "HELPER." The King might be in a business suit, while Esther can wear a pretty sundress and sandals.

PURIMSPIEL

CHARACTERS:

    Storyteller

    Helpers   — *(As many as needed to accommodate the class)*

    Esther

    Mordecai

    Simpleton

    Rabbi

    Old Woman

    King

    Haman

Storyteller: (HE IS DRESSED AS A JESTER AND COMES RUNNING AND TUMBLING ON STAGE) Boys and Girls! Friends and neighbors! Guess what time of year this is?! It is the silliest, happiest time of all! The time for merriment—and parties—and costumes and carnivals! The time for *hamentashen* and *Purimspiel*! Now do you know? That's right, it's Purim! And we must celebrate! So come on, wipe those frowns off your faces and...and...what's that? Did I hear someone say, "What's Purim?" I don't believe my own ears! I'm astounded! I'm flabbergasted! I'm ...I'm...I'm going to tell you the story of Purim and of a lovely Jewish heroine named Esther. Curtain, please! (HE TAKES HOLD OF THE

CENTER OPENING OF THE CURTAIN AND WALKS OFFSTAGE AS THOUGH HE WERE PULLING IT OPEN)

Now, let's see. Hmmmmm. I can't do this all alone. I need some help. I need some *Purimspiel* players. (HE CLAPS HIS HANDS AND COMMANDS) Players! Helpers! Come out here! I need your help! (SEVERAL OTHER ACTORS DRESSED AS JESTERS COME OUT TO HELP WITH THE NARRATION AND THE SET CHANGES)

Helper I: Here we are. How can we help?

Helper II: Yes, how can we h...(HE NOTICES THE AUDIENCE AT THIS POINT) Wow, look at all the people out there! What do they want?

Storyteller: They want to hear a story.

Helper I: Oh, I love to tell stories! Especially "The Wizard of Oz!" That's my favorite! Can I tell that?

Storyteller: Well, they really want to hear the...

Helper I: I just love the part where the witch gets water thrown on her and...

Storyteller: Hold on! We are not going to tell "The Wizard of Oz." They want to know the story of Purim. Can you help me?

Helper II: Maybe we could tell the story of Purim and make it sound like "The Wizard of Oz!"

Helper I: Sure, that's easy. Where do you want to begin?

Storyteller: Well, our best scenery is for the palace scenes, so let's begin our play after Esther has become Queen. But you'd better tell them what happened before that.

Helper III: Oh, I'll tell! Let me! I'm very good at telling stories. You see, once upon a time...

Helper I: Oh, that's boring already. Once upon a time! Every story starts out with "Once upon a time." Can't you be a little more original? Like...A long time ago in a city in Persia called Shushan there lived a small community of Jews. And among this community was a lovely young orphan named...

Helper III: Esther! (HE SMILES BROADLY WITH A SENSE OF ACHIEVEMENT)

Helper II: Ahem! Yes, Esther. Now, Esther was being raised by her elder cousin, a man called...

Helper III: Mordecai! (SMILES)

Helper I: Ahem, yes...Mordecai. Now, Mordecai had heard that the King...

Helper II: King Ahashuerus! (VERY PLEASED WITH HIMSELF...THE OTHER TWO HELPERS GIVE HIM A DIRTY LOOK)

Helpers I & III: (TOGETHER) Ahem!

Helper II: Well, I can tell some, too!

Helpers I & III: Go on.

Helper II: (ALL IN ONE BREATH AND VERY FAST AND AS HE FINISHES, HE RUNS OUT OF BREATH) Well, King Ahashuerus had banished Queen Vashti for refusing to come to a banquet he was giving and so he was looking for a new queen and Mordecai persuaded Esther to try her luck because she was very beautiful and nice, too, and so she did and the King took one look at her and it was love at first sight and he made her the Queen and she went to live in the palace but she never told the King that she was Jewish. Whew! Right?

Helpers I & III: RIGHT!

Storyteller: Very good, except you forgot the part about...(HE WHISPERS TO HELPER II)

Helper II: Oh, yeah.

Helpers I & III: What did he say? What did he say? (HELPER II WHISPERS TO THEM) Oh, he's right. I forgot that part. So I did.

Storyteller: What I reminded them of was that after Esther had become Queen, Mordecai had overheard a plot against the King. He told Esther and she in turn told the King. This made the King even more grateful and in love with Esther and he gave her many beautiful things.

Helper I: Oh, yeah, she lived real nice.

Storyteller: This is where our story picks up. (SPEAKS TO THE HELPERS) Let's have the Queen's chamber scene set up. (THEY GO OFFSTAGE AND RETURN WITH SOME MINIMAL SCENERY, A CUTOUT OF A WINDOW, A BEAUTIFULLY DRAPED CHAIR, ETC. THE WINDOW SHOULD BE PLACED AT AN ANGLE FACING THE AUDIENCE SO THAT ESTHER AND MORDECAI CAN PLAY THE SCENE ON EITHER SIDE OF IT AND BE VISIBLE TO THE AUDIENCE.) Now, we're ready to begin ...or continue actually. Actors! Places, please! (ESTHER COMES ON STAGE AND SITS WITH A BOOK IN HER CHAIR) Action!

Mordecai: (COMES CREEPING TO THE WINDOW. THE LIGHTING SHOULD TRY FOR A NIGHTTIME EFFECT) Esther! (HE WHISPERS HER NAME) Esther!

Esther: Uncle Mordecai! My goodness! What are you doing out there at this time of night?

Mordecai: Oh, Esther, it's terrible, terrible!

Esther: What? What is terrible?

Mordecai: I just overheard.

Esther: What did you overhear?

Mordecai: Oh, it's too horrible.

Esther: What? What is so terrible and horrible?

Mordecai: Haman, the King's advisor...

Esther: Yes, I know Haman is horrible

and mean and nasty, but what has happened to upset you so?

Mordecai: You know how Haman is making everyone bow down to him? Well, he is furious because the Jews won't bow down to him. He has even told the King that the Jews are traitors and are plotting against the kingdom and deserve to die!

Esther: Oh, no! Surely the King won't believe him!

Mordecai: Haman is very convincing and the King is letting him have his way. This very day Haman has cast lots to choose the day upon which we are all to die! It's terrible!

Esther: It's horrible. What can we do?

Mordecai: I don't know! Let's think. (EACH ON EITHER SIDE OF THE WINDOW BEGIN PACING BACK AND FORTH AND CHANTING AS IN "LIONS AND TIGERS AND BEARS, OH, MY!" Hating and killing the Jews, Oh, my! Hating and killing the Jews, Oh, my! (STOPPING SUDDENLY, HE SAYS) I have it! You must go to the King and tell him of this plot. You must tell him that you are also a Jew. It is up to you, Esther, to save your people.

Esther: But, I can't! It is forbidden to go to the King without being summoned first! On pain of death! I cannot! I am afraid.

Mordecai: You must! You are our only

chance! Here, I brought you these. (HE HOLDS UP A PAIR OF SLIPPERS) These slippers belonged to your mother, a brave and courageous woman. Put them on. Think of your mother and know that when you wear these, you are following in her footsteps! They will give you courage, too.

Esther: But the King is not even here in the palace! He has just gone to the summer palace for meetings with his advisors! And he is not due back for many weeks. You must have known that he is gone, Uncle Mordecai.

Mordecai: Oh, dear me! I forgot! In all this uproar, I forgot! What shall we do? What shall we do? (HE THINKS FOR A MOMENT) There is only one thing to be done! You must go to him. Think of a reason that would bring you to him...prepare a banquet and bring it to him and his men...yes! That's it!

Esther: Yes, I will say that I wanted to do something extra special for him, and then, during the banquet I will tell him of Haman's horrible and terrible plot. And then I will tell him about myself. I must be brave. (TAKES A DEEP BREATH) I will leave at once! Which way do I go?

Mordecai: That's easy. Just follow the Hamantash Road!

(HE SINGS TO THE TUNE OF "YELLOW

BRICK ROAD")
>Follow the Hamantash Road,
>Follow the Hamantash Road,
>Follow, follow, follow, follow,
>follow the Hamantash Road.
>Follow the sun from the east to west,
>Hurry dear Esther, there's no time to rest.
>Follow, follow, follow, follow,
>follow the Hamantash Road.

(ESTHER CONTINUES THE SONG)
>I'm off to see my husband
>The wonderful King I have wed.
>He can't refuse to help all the Jews
>Send Haman away instead.
>If ever I needed to see the King
>It's now because I hope he'll bring
>Peace and love and happy days because
>Because of the wonderful things he does.

(ESTHER PUTS ON HER MOTHER'S SHOES AND GOES OFF SINGING: "I'M OFF TO SEE MY HUSBAND, THE WONDERFUL KING I HAVE WED." AS MORDECAI EXITS, THE STORYTELLER ENTERS.)

Storyteller: And off she went down the Hamantash Road in hopes of reaching the King and convincing him to help the Jews. On her way she heard a very happy voice. (AS HE NARRATES, HELPERS REMOVE THE PALACE WINDOW AND CHAIR, PLACING CUTOUTS OF TREES OR VERY LARGE

COLORFUL FLOWERS TO SUGGEST A PATH)

Simpleton: Good mornin', Majesty. And where are you headed this fine and sunny day? (HE IS DRESSED IN ZANY CLOTHING)

Esther: Fine and sunny indeed!

Simpleton: Why are you so sad?

Esther: Why are you so happy?

Simpleton: (SINGS TO THE TUNE OF "IF I ONLY HAD A BRAIN")
I am watering my flowers
To while away the hours
And hope the sun will shine.
I don't have a care or worry
And I'm never in a hurry
Because everything is fine.

Esther: Fine! Aren't you Jewish?

Simpleton: Yes, but I haven't done anything wrong, Majesty!

Esther: Haven't you heard the news?

Simpleton: What news?

Esther: Haman, the King's advisor, wants to kill all the Jews!

Simpleton: Oy! That's incredibously awful! That's monsterbly terrible! That's not even good! Considering I'm a Jew!

Esther: Well, so am I! Why don't you come with me. I'm on my way to the King to ask him for his help.

Simpleton: Hmmmmm. I think I will.

(THEY LINK ARMS AND SING)
   We're off to see (my, her)
      husband
   The wonderful King who (I, she)
      wed.
   He can't refuse to help all the
      Jews
   Send Haman away instead.
   If ever there was a man to
      despise
   It's Haman--he's rotten in
      anyone's eyes,
   Because, because, because,
      because, because
   Because of the horrible things
      he does.

Storyteller: And so Esther and her friend are off to meet the King. They are dancing along the Haman-tash Road until they are stopped by the sound of moaning and groaning.

Rabbi: (HE HAS COME ONTO THE STAGE AND ASSUMED HIS POSITION AS THE STORYTELLER IS TALKING) *Oy, Oy, Oy, Oy!*

Esther: Stop! Listen! Do you hear something?

Rabbi: (MOANING AND GROANING)

Simpleton: Yes, I hear moaning and groaning. Look, there's an old Rabbi. Maybe it's he. (LOOKING AROUND) Especially since I don't see anyone else.

Rabbi: (MOANS AND GROANS EVEN LOUDER)

Esther: (WALKS OVER TO HIM) What's

the matter? Why are you moaning and groaning?

Rabbi: Why are you singing and laughing? Haven't you heard?

Esther: Do you mean about Haman wanting to kill all the Jews?

Rabbi: Yes. *Oyyyyyyy! Vaaaaay!* My heart--it is breaking!

Simpleton: (TO THE AUDIENCE) I'd moan and groan, too, if my heart were breaking.

Rabbi: Young man, stop mumbling! If you have something to say, speak up! My ears aren't so good anymore.

(SINGS TO THE TUNE OF "IF I ONLY HAD A BRAIN")
   I have given up my pulpit
   Because this nasty culprit
   Is treatening all the Jews
   And I fear my heart is breaking
   All the Jews this Haman's taking
   And our heads we'll surely lose!

Esther: Why don't you come with us. We are going to see King Ahashuerus. He is a good and honest man. He will help us.

Rabbi: Why not? Maybe it will make me feel better. I'll try anything. Which way do we go?

Esther: Just follow the Hamantash Road! (REPEAT SONG)

Storyteller: And so the three of them continued on their way until they heard someone crying.

Old Woman: (SHE HAS ASSUMED HER PLACE AND CRIES SOFTLY AS THE STORYTELLER IS TALKING) Woe is me...Woe is me...

Esther: What the matter, old woman?

Old Woman: Oh, it's terrible! I'm so afraid! I heard that Haman is going to kill all the Jews! And I wish I had the courage to do something about it! But I'm so afraid!

(SHE SINGS TO THE TUNE OF "IF I ONLY HAD A BRAIN")
Oh, I know I am a coward
And I wish I had the power
To help my fellow Jews.
But I'm quivering and quaking
And my insides have been
    shaking
Since I heard the awful news.

All: You can do something about it!

Esther: You can come with us to see the King! We are going to ask him to help us. (THEY ALL LINK ARMS AND SKIP ALONG TO THE MUSIC OF "YELLOW BRICK ROAD" AS THE STORYTELLER SPEAKS)

Storyteller: And so Esther and her friends went together to seek the help of King Ahashuerus. They continued on their way until they reached their destination.

Esther: Well, here we are. Oh, dear me. I'm so nervous!

Storyteller: Esther did feel very reluctant to face the King. But then she remembered what she had on her feet and the wise and wonderful words of Mordecai.

Mordecai: (OFFSTAGE VOICE) Put on these shoes. They belonged to your mother who was a very courageous woman. Whenever you are afraid, just look at these shoes. They will give you courage. (ESTHER AND HER FRIENDS COME DOWNSTAGE CENTER AND GRASP HANDS TO SUMMON ALL THEIR COURAGE AS HELPERS REMOVE THE PATH BRINGING ON AND PLACING A THRONE UPSTAGE CENTER. THE KING ENTERS, SITS ON THE THRONE AND SPEAKS)

King: Send in the Queen!

Esther: (THE SOUND OF THE KING'S COMMAND STARTLES THE GROUP OF FRIENDS AND THEY SEPARATE. THEN ESTHER WALKS TOWARD THE KING.)

Esther: My good husband and King. Please forgive this intrusion. You see, I thought that perhaps you might be so bored just talking business all this time so I decided to liven up your day with a banquet.

King: My dear Esther, I could never be angry with you. You have brought me nothing but happiness. I am pleased that you thought of me. But why the long face? You seem upset. And who are these people that you have brought with you? I do not recognize them.

Esther: If it please Your Majesty, these are my friends. They have helped me on my way here today.

King: Then they are my friends, too. Welcome, friends. (THEY ALL BOW)

Esther: There is something else, too, my King.

King: Yes? Why do you hesitate so?

Esther: Your Majesty, there is something I have never told you about myself. But something I must tell you now.

King: A secret? From me? But surely it can't be so terrible as to make you so nervous and frightened. What is it?

Esther: I am a Jew, Your Majesty. And so are my friends here. We have heard that your friend and advisor, Haman, has filled your head with all kinds of terrible lies about my people, and that now he has cast lots to select a day on which to kill us all.

King: But not you, Esther. You are the Queen.

Esther: Your Majesty, if all the Jews are to die, I want no special favors. I must die with my people.

King: NO! I will not allow it! I did not realize that Haman had gone this far! He has taken too much into his own hands. He shall pay for this. He, not the Jews, will hang on the gallows that he has erected. You shall be my Queen and you and your people shall be free to live in peace in my kingdom.

Esther: Oh, thank you, Your Majesty! Thank you.

Friends: Thank you, sire.

King: Everyone, come here!!! (THE HELPERS AND STORYTELLER AND ANY OTHER EXTRAS CAN ENTER AT THIS POINT) Bring Haman to me. Put him under arrest and spread the news...As long as I am King, the Jews will live in peace and freedom. And on this day, Haman will hang for his wickedness.

All: (SING TO THE TUNE OF "DING DONG, THE WITCH IS DEAD")
Ding, dong, find Haman cause
He has broken all the laws.
Ding, dong, we must find
Haman now...

(THEY ALL WALK OUT INTO THE AUDIENCE ASKING EVERYONE: "HAVE YOU SEEN HAMAN?" DO YOU KNOW WHERE HAMAN IS?" SUDDENLY, ONE PERSON SPOTS HAMAN SNEAKING ACROSS THE STAGE AND YELLS.)

Person: There he is! Grab him! (THEY ALL RUN BACK ONTO THE STAGE. TWO PEOPLE BEGIN TO DRAG HIM OFF.)

Haman: Wait! You are mistaken! I'm the good guy! I...I... (HE IS TAKEN OFF STAGE. THE REMAINING PEOPLE ON STAGE BEGIN SINGING AND ARE JOINED BY THE TWO WHO

HAVE REMOVED HAMAN.)
>   Ding, dong, Haman's dead
>   The Jews will live, will live
>   instead,
>   Ding, dong, the wicked Haman's
>   dead!
>   He's gone where the bad men go,
>   Below, below, below.
>   Yoho, let's all rejoice and sing
>   The King is kind and
>   Ding, dong, old Haman's dead,
>   Jews will live, live instead.
>   It's been said...the wicked
>   Haman's dead!

(CURTAIN)

The Freedom Birds

Grades 5-8

Adapted with permission from the story "The Breakfast of the Birds" by Judah Steinberg, published by The Jewish Publication Society of America, 1917.

PRODUCTION NOTES

This play may be performed as a pulpit presentation during a Friday night service or as a proscenium production with more elaborate setting and lights. To accommodate a larger group, the narration may be given in shorter segments to storytellers, and a whole chorus of birds may be choreographed to dance in the last scene.

The use of exciting costumes will attract the audience and enliven this production, particularly if it is performed on the pulpit. Make two fantastic bird heads and very large wings from construction paper. When worn with brightly matched leotards and tights, these will create a wonderful visual effect. Dress the storyteller colorfully in jeans rolled up to the knee, very loud knee socks and suspenders over colorful, long sleeved T-shirts. Add a floppy, pointed hat made from felt with bells at the tip. The taskmaster, all in green, can also wear a green plastic helmet that stands very high on the head and comes down over the eyes, making him appear to loom over the slaves. Do the rest of the costuming and makeup in a very stylized manner. The mother and father can wear long sleeved black turtleneck shirts and white sheets draped like togas in the opposite direction on each. Both should use white mime face makeup with large teardrops painted on opposite cheeks. The children can be dressed like the parents, but in different colored shirts under their togas. Their makeup should also be white-face, but without the teardrop. Draw very wide eyes and eyelashes instead.

THE FREEDOM BIRDS: A PASSOVER TALE

CHARACTERS:

Narrator	Boy
Taskmaster	Sister
Man	Bird I
Woman	Bird II

Narrator: Good evening. Let me introduce myself. I am the storyteller. I make my living going from town to town, city to city telling stories. I stopped here because it is Passover time and I have a wonderful story to tell you--a tale about the true meaning of the Exodus, a tale called, "The Freedom Birds." And now before we begin, I'd like you to meet our cast of characters:

(AS EACH CHARACTER IS ANNOUNCED, HE/SHE COMES OUT TO THE CENTER OF THE STAGE, IN CHARACTER, AND ACKNOWLEDGES THE AUDIENCE, THEN RETURNS TO HIS/HER OFFSTAGE POSITION)

First we have the evil taskmaster who unmercifully prodded the Hebrew slaves to work far beyond their abilities. Then we have a Hebrew bondsman whose life consisted of toiling for Pharaoh without any hope of pay or freedom; his wife who spent her days cooking the meager portions for her family and bringing it to the fields for her husband; their children who were left at home lonely and afraid and who found whatever happiness they could in being in the sunshine and talking to the animals. And our heroes, the birds...the birds... (EXASPERATED, CALLING) The birds! Oh, well, you'll meet them later. They must be off flying around somewhere. You see, they don't have to stay here. They can go wherever they please. Well, now we are ready to begin. PLACES, PLEASE! PLACES!

Our story begins at the break of day...any day...for all days were the same for the Hebrews in Egypt. There was no day of rest. As soon as the sun came up, the taskmaster was at the door, his whip in hand, signaling the beginning of another day.

Taskmaster: (BANGING ON THE DOOR) Arise! You have rested long enough! There is work to be done...straw to be gathered...bricks to be baked. Get up, you lazy good-for-nothing!

Man: Yes. Yes, master, I am coming. I am just finishing my meal.

Taskmaster: Enough, Hebrew dog, we are wasting precious daylight. Be quick, or you will taste this instead! (RAISES STICK)

Woman: Go, my husband. Do not anger the taskmaster or we will all be made to suffer. I will bring you food later. Go quickly or he will double your workload and you will end up just like Gildar who became crippled from the work and was put to death because he could no longer do Pharaoh's bidding.

Man: You are right. I will go. What else can I do? (EXITS WITH TASK-MASTER BEHIND)

Woman: Why must we live like this? What can we do? Nothing! Our days will begin and end in slavery. There is no hope. (BEGINS TO CRY) My poor children. (EXITS)

Boy: Come, sister. Let us go out in the sun. It is too sad in here. I cannot stand to see mother cry. Let's go and see if any animals want to play.

Sister: All right. And here are some crumbs to feed the birds. If we remember to feed them then they will come back again to play.

Boy: Oh, look! They must know somehow that we have food...here they come!

Sister: Over here, birds! Over here! (MUSIC OR BIRD SOUNDS CAN BE HEARD AS THE BIRDS COME GAILY DANCING DOWN THE AISLE FROM THE BACK OF THE HOUSE)

Boy: Oh, you are such a pretty bird. Here, have some crumbs.

Sister: Where do you come from, birds, and where do you go when you leave us?

Bird I: Away...away...we fly away
Whenever we're in the mood
To lands of rivers and
rolling hills
And always plenty of food.

Boy: Oh, I wish I could see such a land one day.

Sister: Well, we can't. We can't go anywhere. We must stay here. And you will grow up to bake bricks for Pharaoh and I will marry and spend my days carrying food to the fields--just like our mother.

Boy: Here, birds, have some more food and tell us about these lands that you visit.

Bird II: Thank you...thank you
We're as grateful as can be
'Tis a pity hearts so
kind are
Bound in slavery.

Sister: Aren't you slaves?

Bird I: A slave? A slave?
Not we...not we!
We fly wherever we care to.
We're free, my dears,
we're free!

Boy: This freedom you sing of...what's it like? Is it good?

Bird II: GOOD! Listen well, lest it
be forgot
There is no good where
freedom's not!

Bird I: To be free...to be free
Is what you should be
For in the cage, my little friends
Dwells only misery.

Boy: You are right. We are living in a cage. I think I would like to try some of this freedom you talk about.

Sister: I don't know. It sounds so scary. You have to find your own food and build your own nests, I mean, your own houses...it all depends on you...I don't know. I have to think about it.

Bird II: Ah, once you have tasted liberty
You'll know for evermore
Better to hunger in freedom
Than to feast in slavery's store.

Narrator: (AS THE NARRATOR IS SPEAKING, THE MOTHER AND FATHER RETURN TO THE STAGE AND THE CHILDREN WALK UP INTO THE SCENE) And so the children went home and spoke with their parents about this thing called "freedom."

Man: Yes, my children, freedom is a precious thing...more precious than all Pharaoh's gold.

Woman: It is something to think about ...it will give us hope.

Boy: No! No! The birds have said that thinking about it is just the beginning, but only in striving for it will we have any chance of finding it.

Man: There are rumors of a man among us, a stranger from Midian, who claims to be a Hebrew. He calls himself Moses. He also speaks of freedom and begs us to unite and leave Egypt. He claims to speak the words of God. They say he is going to go before Pharaoh himself and ask him to let our people go.

Woman: Oh, no. I am afraid. What would become of us? Where would we go? At least here, even as slaves, we know what exists for us. We have food. We live!

Birds: (OVERHEARING THE SCENE FROM THEIR PERCH)
Better to hunger with the free
Than eat the feast of slavery
Freedom is precious and does
   not come cheap
Today you sacrifice...tomorrow
   you reap!

Narrator: (AS THE NARRATOR SPEAKS, EXTRAS ENTER ONTO THE STAGE AREA FOR THE FINAL SCENE) And so it came to pass that the children of Israel did unite and, with Moses as their leader, left the land of their bondage. But as the days wore on, the people grew very hungry, for there was little to eat. Soon there began thoughts of returning to Egypt.

Hebrew: You see, I knew it. We never should have come. We will starve to death in this desert!

Hebrew: Maybe you're right. I don't know. Maybe we should turn back...

Narrator: The birds who had been following along and heard this frightening talk quickly gathered together and in a language no human ear could understand, decided what must be done. (AT THIS POINT A CHOREOGRAPHED DANCE OF BIRDS COULD BE INTRODUCED) Soon a host of quail fell from the skies.

All: Look! We have food! Food at last! Where did this come from? We do not have to turn back after all...

Narrator: But the children knew that it was their friends, the birds, who had seen their plight and had sacrificed themselves in the cause of freedom. And even today on *Shabbat Shirah*, the Sabbath on which is read the victory song of Moses--the Song of the Reed Sea, we also read the *Sidrah* of the Quail--to remember how the birds kept the Israelites from turning back.

From Freedom to Independence

Grades 5-12

PRODUCTION NOTES

This production is not so much a play as a dramatic reading, although it is best if the lines are memorized. Pacing and variety of tempo and pitch in line delivery are especially important in this type of presentation. Such variation is needed to avoid the possibility of monotony, since there is little action. It will also ensure that what is being said can be easily understood by the audience.

For costuming, the ancient Israelites can wear robes and headdresses, while the modern Israelis can wear jeans, shorts and short sleeved white shirts. Some can also wear *kibbutz* hats, if desired.

FROM FREEDOM TO INDEPENDENCE

CHARACTERS:
- Group of Ancient Israelites
- Group of Modern Israelis
- Israelite Narrator
- Israeli Narrator
- Moses
- Aaron
- Ben Gurion

(AFTER THE CAST IS INTRODUCED, THE MUSIC FROM "EXODUS" BEGINS AND THE STUDENTS APPROACH THE *BIMAH*. THE ANCIENT ISRAELITES STAND GROUPED ON ONE SIDE, THE NEW ISRAELIS ON THE OTHER.)

Ancients: And God took us out of the land of Egypt--out of the house of bondage and showed us the Promised Land.

Israelis: And we were liberated from the ghettos of Europe and the concentration camps of Germany--and began our exodus once again to the Promised Land.

All: Passover--a celebration of liberation--of freedom.

Narrator-Ancient: The Book of Exodus tells how Moses led some 600,000 adults and children out of Egypt. Our people had lived there for 430 years.

Narrator-Israeli: Ben Gurion had helped to create a modern nation of just over 600,000 Jews after 430 years of Turkish and British rule.

Ancient I: And the children of Israel were living in Egypt for 430 years as slaves and were treated harshly. But the more they were afflicted, the more they grew until their numbers became a threat to the Pharaoh of Egypt.

Israeli I: For 2000 years the Jews of Europe, North Africa and the Near East dreamed of returning some day to the ancient land of their ancestors--like them, they lived in bondage, the subjects of new Pharaohs.

Moses: Moses is my name. And the Lord spoke unto me and commanded me to take my people out of this land of bondage and into a land flowing with milk and honey.

Ancient II: And Moses and Aaron, his brother, went to the elders. And Aaron told the people what had happened.

Aaron: The Lord spoke to my brother and said that He has not forgotten us. He will take us out of this land and He has given Moses some signs to convince you.

Ancient III: Look, the rod--it is turned into a snake!

Ancient IV: And back again into a rod!

Ancient V: And behold, the skin on Moses' hand--it has turned white and dead looking...and now it has turned clear again.

Ancient VI: I am convinced it is the Lord's wish. Let us go to Pharaoh and tell him...

All: Let my people go!

Narrator-Israeli: And thousands of years later, there was another man--a new Moses--a man with dreams of taking his people out of foreign lands and back to Zion--David Ben Gurion.

Israeli I: The Holocaust of World War II was threatening.

Israeli II: Jews were being beaten and shot. Synagogues and stores were being burned.

Israeli III: Our people once again lived under a terrible oppression.

Israeli IV: But in Palestine there lived a man who tried to free these people.

Ben Gurion: David Ben Gurion is my name--I live in Palestine, I work the land in Palestine, but I dream of the day when it will be called Israel once again. I see what is happening to my people and I must fight for their freedom.

Israeli V: David, we must go to London, to the Colonial office and apply for immigration certificates for our people...

Israeli VI: We must tell them...

All: Let my people go!

Narrator-Ancient: And Moses went to Pharaoh and told him that the Lord had commanded him to let the people of Israel go free.

Moses: But Pharaoh was stubborn--he would not listen to me.

Narrator-Ancient: But God performed many miracles for the children of Israel.

All: And at last they were free--free to enter the Promised Land.

Narrator-Israeli: And during the Holocaust, when the world still refused the Jews a safe place of their own, Ben Gurion spoke to these new Pharaohs...

Ben Gurion: If it is not within your power to put a stop to the slaughter --why do you not let us fight for the blood of our millions of people and allow us to take up arms as a nation--as Jews under a Jewish flag?

Narrator-Israeli: And again God did not forget the children of Israel-- and performed a wonderful miracle!

All: In 1948, the State of Israel was proclaimed.

Moses: I was not as lucky as you, Ben Gurion. I did not live to see our people in the Promised Land.

Ben Gurion: That is true. I lived to

see our people have a homeland of their own once again--my dreams came true.

Ancients: We must never forget that we were once slaves in the land of Egypt.

Israelis: We must never forget the six million.

All: We must never forget that God is One. We must never forget God's wonderful miracles. And at this joyous Passover season, we thank God by saying:

(ALL RECITE *SHEHECHEYANU*)
Baruch atah adonai eloheynu melech ha-olam shehecheyanu v'ki-y'manu v'higi-anu lazman hazeh.

Blessed Art Thou, O Lord
  Our God,
King of the Universe Who has
  kept us alive and sustained
  us and brought us to this
  season.

(SING *"ADDIR HU"*)

So Young to Die: The Story of Hannah Senesh
Grades 7-12

Adapted with the permission of Catherine and Giora Senesh from HANNAH SENESH: HER LIFE AND DIARY, Marta Cohn, Translator. N.Y.: Schocken Books, 1973.

PRODUCTION NOTES

During that dark period of history known as the Holocaust, where evil forces sought to destroy our people, there arose a few whose acts of heroism and valor in fighting the evil are awesome.

Although Anne Frank's diary reveals so well the thoughts and feelings of a young person caught in the hopelessness of the times, we look to another diary which, when combined with her letters and the memories of friends and relatives, reveals the story of a most remarkable, dedicated heroine of the Jewish people--the story of Hannah Senesh.

Hannah Senesh was a girl like many that we know today--charming, restless, an exceptional student, but very much a teen-ager at the time we first come to know her in 1934 at the age of 13.

The action of the play begins in the interior of Hannah's home in Budapest, an obviously well kept home as suggested by a white lace cloth and silver candlesticks on the table. Because of the change of scenes, a presentational approach is best, using either spotlighting or blocking to call attention to the speaker.

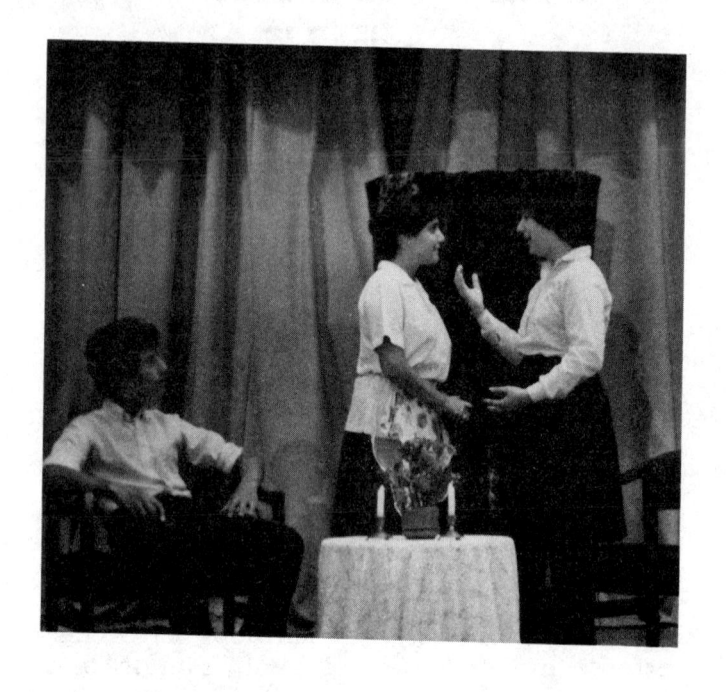

SO YOUNG TO DIE:
THE STORY OF HANNAH SENESH

CHARACTERS:

    Mama — *A handsome, loving woman in early middle age*

    Hannah — *Vivacious, full of life, aging from 13–23*

    George — *Her brother*

    Eva
    Betsy — *Her friends*

    Reuven
    Yoel — *Friends from Palestine, part of the mission*

    Narrator

Hannah: Mother! Mother! Guess what? Maria's mother asked me to tutor Maria six hours a week and she's going to pay me. Now I can pay for dancing classes and skating lessons with my own money. Perhaps I'll even buy a season ticket to the ice rink.

Mama: How wonderful, Hannah. But you must not give so much time as to let your studies slide.

Hannah: Mama, don't worry. Don't worry, all my marks are good. Only, I have to improve a little in French. And Mama, guess what? Today we got a new teacher and he is a writer and he knew Papa.

He recognized my name and asked if I were any relation to the playwright, Bela Senesh.

Mama: Ah, Hannah...He was not only famous in Budapest, but his comedies were performed in many countries. They would have been performed at the National Theatre—if he had not been Jewish.

Hannah: Mama, I don't understand... why does that make a difference? Why?

Mama: Why? For the same reason they make us pay three times the normal tuition for you to go to the private school...even though you are among the brightest there and should have a scholarship...In fact, I have decided to go to the school and speak to them about it...We may not be able to continue the school much longer.

George: (ENTERS) Hello, I'm home... I'm going to go to the Indoor Pool this evening, Mama...there is a match between Hungary and America ...all my friends are going...it's going to be very exciting.

Hannah: Mama, can we go to the films tonight? "The Scarlet Pimpernel" is playing. We read it in my English class and I would love to see it... It has Leslie Howard in it.

Mama: Yes, yes, that would be nice.

George: How is your play writing coming along, Hannah?

Hannah: How do you know I want to write plays?...George! You were reading my diary! You did...George, I could kill you!! Mama, do something.

George: Well, you left it sitting around and...

Mama: George, I'm ashamed of you... that is private and...

George: I didn't read very much...I'm sorry, Hannah, really I am.

Hannah: Well, I do want to write, I think about it all the time. It is such a marvelous feeling to write something well! (BLACKOUT)

Narrator: And write she did, all her thoughts and feelings in her diary, and in her poetry and plays as well. Through her writings you could feel her grow and mature, toy with new ideas, grapple with her feelings and watch her as a few years later, she became aware of--and then aflame with--one burning ideal...Zionism!

(A FEW YEARS LATER. HANNAH, EVA AND BETSY ARE TALKING.)

Hannah: Oh, Eva, I know this is right for me. My whole life I have felt like a Hungarian, but now I know that I am an outcast in the land where I was born! I am constantly feeling humiliated and angry! Why should I have to feel like that?

Eva: You just have to learn to ignore

things like that. Don't be crazy, Hannah, you have everything a person could want—a beautiful home, a wonderful school to go to, many friends and family and summers by the lake...

Hannah: But don't you understand, I have finally found out who I am! At last I have an identity and I never want to be made to feel ashamed of it!

Betsy: Oh, Hannah, you're so silly. We know who you are, too. You're Hannah Senesh, 17 years old and already very well thought of in the community for your brain and your talent.

Hannah: Oh, but I am so much more than that. I am a Zionist! For the first time I feel solid ground beneath my feet and a goal worth striving for!

George: (ENTERS, HAVING OVERHEARD HER STATEMENT) You're right, Hannah. Here it is 1938! Modern times! An enlightened era...for everyone except the Jews, that is. Zionism is Jewry's solution to its problem!

Hannah: Oh, George, I love you for saying that...I am so happy that you feel this way, too. There is so much work to be done in Palestine...and I want to be a part of it.

George: And I, too, when I finish the University in France...

Mama: (ENTERS) You, too, what?

Hannah: We were talking of Palestine, Mama. We want to go there to work the land, to feel proud of our Jewishness, to feel at home, not alien! Surely you, too, have felt how things are worsening around here for Jews...

George: The situation is rapidly deteriorating, Mama. A new Jewish law is going into effect--The New Land Reform, they call it. The government has no right to take away land owned by Jews, but they do it anyway. We have no rights!!!

Mama: Yes, you are right, times are distressing. Come, George, we will go into the garden and talk about this idea of yours. (MAMA AND GEORGE GO OFF. HANNAH, EVA AND BETSY REMAIN.)

Eva: It sounds very frightening to me. A strange land far away. How big is it? What kind of houses do they have? What kind of food is there? You are very brave to even think of it!

Hannah: These days I can think of nothing else.

Eva: Well, let me tell you about the party I went to the other night... There was the cutest boy...

Hannah: Frankly, I can't help thinking how nice it would be if all the money spent on the party would have been put in the Blue Box instead.

Narrator: What can one say of Hannah Senesh...that she was determined, YES! A hard worker, without question! Idealistic, absolutely. But above and beyond all of this, she had ability to understand the reality of the day when others chose to ignore it. The year is 1939. The war has begun and Hannah is leaving for Palestine.

Hannah: Eva, Betsy, I'm going to miss you. I promise to write.

Betsy: Take some pictures, OK? And send them to us...so we can see what this place looks like...what's it called?

Hannah: Nahalal—it's a girls agricultural school and I'm going to be doing all kinds of intellectual things like feeding the chickens and milking the cows and planting the vegetables...and building a country!

Betsy: You make it sound so glamorous!

Hannah: Glamorous, no. Necessary, yes! You have heard about the newest Jewish law, haven't you? Now they are legislating how many Jews will be allowed in commerce and industry. No Jew is allowed to be a lawyer or a teacher or a judge! What will be next?

Eva: My father says this will pass... that things will get better. There have always been times of anti-

Semitism.

Hannah: Eva, my dear friend...I am a good person and so are you. I have hopes and dreams for my future--we all do. I have the right to be able to fulfill them and so do you...but here in my native country, they deny me this.

Betsy: But you were born here...this is where you have always lived.

Hannah: You think you are a citizen but the new laws say otherwise. I am going to build a country where no law can take away my rights...where all Jews will be welcome.

Narrator: By the end of September 1939, at the age of 18, Hannah was writing letters to her mother from the Nahalal Agricultural School in Palestine.

Mama: I still have all of Hannah's letters. I don't know why I kept them all. I guess I thought they were all so beautifully written, said so much, that there was so much of her in each one, that I couldn't bring myself to throw them away. Here, this one was written from Nahalal right after she got there...

Hannah: "Dearest Mother, Today I must write in Hungarian as there are such an endless number of things to write about, so many impressions to record, that I can't possibly cope with them all in Hebrew yet.

I would like to be able to express on this day before Yom Kippur, the Day of Atonement, all that I want to say. I would like to be able to record what these first days in Palestine mean to me, because I have been here four days. I am in Nahalal, in *Eretz*. I am home."

Mama: That was in September 1939. She kept a diary there, too. And her friends were kind enough to bring it to me after the war. She had her father's gift for words... there was no doubt of that. How she poured her heart out on paper. Sometimes I think the diary was her best friend. This entry was from September 1941...

(AS EACH PERSON BEGINS HIS/HER LETTER OR MEMORY, HE/SHE TAKES A PLACE ON STAGE AND REMAINS UNTIL THE CURTAIN)

Mother: (BEGINS ALONE: HANNAH BEGINS SPEAKING WITH MAMA AT THE UNDERLINED WORDS AND GRADUALLY BEGINS SPEAKING ALONE) "It's the eve of Rosh Hashanah, the Jewish New Year. Two years have already passed since I left home. Two years away from my mother, my home, from my brother. I've been away three years, and I've lived two years in the Land. <u>If I could, I would write a few words to my mother.</u> I have so much to tell her. But because of the war it is impossible. It's hard to know what I'd talk to her about were we to meet now. I would tell her about these years, about my dreams, my plans, my anxieties. I would tell her how I felt yesterday. I was so desperately depressed that I cried. I felt I was faced with two possibilities: to seek personal happiness and shut my eyes to the faults in my surroundings, or else to invest my efforts in the difficult and devastating war for the things I deem good and proper. But I don't think the decision is up to me. I feel hidden traits within me will determine my course of action. Dear God, if You have kindled a fire in my heart, allow me to burn that which should be burned in my house--the House of Israel. And as You have given me an all seeing eye and an all hearing ear, give me, as well, the strength to scourge, to caress, to uplift. And grant that these not be empty phrases, but a credo to my life."

George: Hannah wrote to me, too. And whenever I read it to myself I ask, Why? Why is someone so good, so selfless, allowed to die? Where's the sense? And yet, maybe the answer is in her letter...

"Dear George, Sometimes one writes letters one does not intend sending. Letters one must write without asking oneself, I wonder whether this will ever reach its destination. Day after tomorrow I am starting something new. Perhaps it's madness, perhaps it's fantastic, perhaps it's dangerous, perhaps one in a hundred thousand pays with his life. Don't ask questions. You'll eventually know what it's about. I wonder, will you understand? I wonder, will you believe that it is more than just a childish wish for adventure, more than youthful romanticism that attracted me? There are events without which one's life becomes unimportant, a worthless toy; and there are times when one is commanded to do something, even at the price of one's own life."

She wrote this letter at the beginning of her parachute training. I found out that Hannah had been training with the Palmach. Why did they want her to exhibit such strength, such devotion to a cause, such enthusiasm and optimism that others flock to her the way a moth clings to the light. She was like that...always...but as for joining the parachute group...

Hannah: I had to do it. I was suddenly struck by the idea of going to Hungary. I felt I must be there during these days in order to help organize youth immigration, and also to get my mother out. My mother...I miss her so...and I worry about her constantly...The reports coming to us of what is happening in Europe are so frightening...I have a hopeful plan to get my mother out and bring her here, at any cost.

Reuven: I had the privilege of serving on the same mission with Hannah during the war, spending months with her, slogging through the land after we were dropped and remaining with her until that terrible day she crossed the Hungarian border and, betrayed by some Yugoslav partisans, fell into Nazi hands. She was always happy and cheerful, joking with us, yet not taking her mind off the mission, making suggestions and planning details for action. Her changes in mood astounded me. One moment she would be rolling with laughter, the next aflame with the fervor of the mission. I felt that a kind of divine spark must be burning in the depths of her being, motivating her. She, more than any of the others, showed a lack of fear of jumping. During those dreadful, difficult moments when my heart would pound with trepidation before a jump, I would think of Hannah, her comforting words of encouragement, and feel relaxed, reassured. She was fearless, and none of us was as positive as she that our mission would succeed, and that we would be able to rescue the Hungarian Jewish children waiting to be smuggled out to safety...When on the night of March 13, 1944, we were told to get ready to leave, she was overjoyed. She sang the whole way back to the village and made us sing along with her. That song, in the course of our mission, became our group's theme song.

Yoel: I was part of the mission, too. But we were all more than just fellow workers...I can't begin to tell you how the months of training, the shared fears and hopes created a friendship, a closeness, a love for each other rarely found in normal times. But these were not normal times. Well, neither one of us ever reached our destination--a prearranged rendezvous site...we met instead inside Gestapo prison. We managed to find a way to pass messages back and forth and I found that she had suffered dreadful tortures, but she didn't want to talk about them. Only the tooth missing from her mouth was testimony to what they had done to her in an attempt to find out our radio code. But she never told them. They even brought her mother to the prison and threatened to torture her, but...

Mama: But Hannah still would not betray the children she so desperately wanted to help...No one can possibly know the torment that went on inside of Hannah. Ours was a very close relationship, maybe because her father died when she was so young and she had only me...I don't know...I think you could understand better if I read you a poem Hannah once wrote, when she was only 12 years old. It's just called, "Mother."

> If the world offered a reward
> A laurel for patience and love
> One person alone would be worthy:
> Mother.
>
> Let there be thanks in your heart
> And on your lips a prayer,
> Whenever you hear that most beautiful word:
> Mother.

When she saw me in the prison, all she could do was beg me to forgive her. "Forgive me, Mother," she pleaded. "I had to do what I did." I found it very hard to understand what she was doing...why she was willing to sacrifice herself...what drove her to do this. For some unexplained reason they released me unharmed and I was able to visit Hannah for a time...and then the bombings and air raids began and I was unable to leave the house. When I finally was able to go to the prison to see Hannah...it was too late. Instead, they handed me these scraps of paper...found in the pocket of her dress after they shot her...she was writing even in her cell...and even then her love of Palestine was always with her. Here is one that was written before her mission and expresses so well all that she lived for: "To die... so young to die...no, no, not I."

> I love the warm sunny skies
> Light, songs, shining eyes
> I want no war, no battle cry
> No, no, not I.
>
> But if it must be that I live
>   today
> With blood and death on every
>   hand
> Praised be He for the grace,
>   I'll say
> To live, if I should die this
>   day
> Upon your soil, my home,
>   my land.

My poor Hannah, so loving, so full of life, so dedicated to the Jewish people and to *Eretz Yisrael*...She may not have died upon the soil she loved so well, but she was finally buried there and there she will rest forever.

Stranger in the Land: The Story of Ruth

Grades 5-8

PRODUCTION NOTES

This play was written to accommodate a large group. The narration is spoken by a chorus, although parts may be assigned for various lines or verses to add variety to the delivery. It should be given at an exciting fast paced clip.

The play can be as elaborate as desired and performed on any type of stage, including the pulpit, using no scenery and only a few props to suggest the various scenes. Group the chorus facing the audience on stairs or risers which lead to the pulpit. They may stand to recite and sit when the scene on the pulpit begins to play.

STRANGER IN THE LAND: THE STORY OF RUTH

CHARACTERS:

    Ruth

    Orpah

    Naomi

    Boaz

    Man in the Field

    Man at the Gate

    Chorus

(PROLOGUE)

Chorus: We've a story to tell and we can't wait to say it,
It's a story of love and the courage to obey it,
It's the tale of the power of loyalty and truth,
It's a story of a stranger,
It's the story of Ruth.
With an ending that's happy and a moral, too
You'll find out for yourself when we're all through.

Now our story takes place a long time ago,
About eleven hundred fifty before the common era,
That's way before the kings of Israel lived,
But a long time after Moses and Pharaoh.

There was a drought in the
    land of Judah then,
It hadn't rained for years.
And the crops dried up and
    the people were hungry,
Filled with doubts and fears.

But Elimelech said, "To heck
    with all this,
We'll starve if we stay much
    longer.
I'll take my sons and Naomi,
    my wife,
We'll go to Moab and we'll
    grow stronger."

Now that took courage cause
    it wasn't exactly
Like driving from Cleveland
    to L.A.
They'd be outsiders and the
    people weren't friendly,
They were mean and warlike,
    some say.

But people are people
    wherever they live,
And Elimelech knew this was
    true.
So he took his family and
    opened a business,
And he prospered and both
    his sons grew.

But then—oh, dear, (sniff)
    Elimelech died,
And the boys married girls
    who weren't Jewish.
But what else could they do
    living in a strange land,
Their own kind were very

fewish.

As if this wasn't enough
trouble and grief,
You could cry when you hear
what comes next,
Both her sons died leaving
childless widows,
And Naomi was bereaved and
perplexed.

Where should she go—what
should she do?
Hers was a desperate plight.
With no sons to inherit—
she'd lost everything,
For a woman alone had no
rights.

At a time like this, she
needed a family,
Some relatives to stand
behind her.
So she decided to go back to
the land of Judah,
And this is where we find
her...

SCENE I: On the Trail

Naomi: (CARRYING SACKS OF BELONGINGS) Ruth—Orpah—you have come far enough with me—you have seen me more than halfway back to Judah—to my city of Bethlehem—now you must return to your own people. May the Lord keep faith with you and may He grant each of you security in the home of a new husband.

Orpah: Oh, no, mother Naomi, we will return with you to your people.

Naomi: Orpah--what can you be thinking of? You are a Moabitess. Surely you know it would not be easy for you--you will be outcasts--strangers in my land--as I was in yours.

Ruth: We know, my Mother, but we love you. We have shared much with you, including our grief--we do not wish to leave you now.

Naomi: My daughters, my love for you is as great as if you were my own. That is why I am urging you to return to your own land. You are still young--you can marry again --have children--have sons to care for you in your old age--a woman alone is despised.

Orpah: We will find husbands in your land.

Naomi: My people do not like to marry outsiders. Yours will be a difficult lot. Don't you see--with me, your future is so unsure. You must return to the people who know you and worship your own gods.

Orpah: Yes, I can see you are right. Ruth, I am afraid for my future, both our futures. She is right--we must return to Moab.

Ruth: You must do what you feel is right--but as for me--I must stay with Naomi. She is my family. Goodbye, Orpah.

Orpah: Goodbye--goodbye, Naomi.

Naomi: Goodbye, my daughter. Ruth, you must go with her, back to your people and the worship of your gods.

Ruth: Please do not urge me to desert you and go back. Where you go, I will go and where you stay, I will stay. Your people shall be my people and your God, my God. Where you die, I will die and there I will be buried. I swear a solemn oath before God: Nothing but death shall divide us.

Chorus:
On they walked to Bethlehem city,
In need of charity, not wanting pity.
With downcast eyes, Ruth walked beside,
Her doubts and fears she tried to hide.

As they entered into the market square,
Naomi's friends spied her walking there.
She was surprised they even recognized her,
For the years of sorrow had all but disguised her.

Her friends all helped situate the two,
But they couldn't hang around,
They had too much to do.
Everyone was busy and with good reason,

'Cause in Bethlehem it was
harvest season.

SCENE II: At the **Market**

(SEVERAL WOMEN OF THE CHORUS ASCEND THE STAGE AND PLAY THE SCENE)

Woman I: Oh, Naomi—we're so happy you've come back.

Woman II: It's been so long—we want to hear all about Moab—I've heard stories...

Woman III: They are supposed to be barbarians there—I'd be so afraid.

Woman IV: No one knew if you were alive or dead—I mean, living in that place...

Naomi: I'll tell you all about my years in Moab—and of how the Lord has seen fit to bring disaster on me. But first, I must secure a place to stay for me and my daughter-in-law, Ruth.

Woman I: We will help you, Naomi—you are one of us. We are happy to have you back.

Woman II: And we will bring you food, too—until you have become established.

Woman III: Thanks to the Almighty—we have had plentiful harvests. Things have gone well with us the last several years here in Judah. We will help you. (WOMEN RETURN TO CHORUS)

Chorus: But they couldn't expect help forever,
They had to survive of their own endeavor.
So Ruth went off to the fields to glean,
And while she was there--by Boaz was seen.

SCENE III: In the Fields

(BOAZ AND A MAN ENTER FROM THE AUDIENCE AND BEGIN SPEAKING AS THEY ARE WALKING ONTO THE STAGE)

Boaz: Who is that dark haired young girl out there working so hard? I have not seen her before.

Man: She is a Moabitess who has just come back with Naomi. She even asked permission if she might glean in your fields, Boaz--and she has been on her feet with hardly a moment's rest from daybreak to now.

Boaz: Ah--I have heard the story of this young girl who wishes herself an uncertain fate in a strange land rather than abandon her mother-in-law. Bring her over to me. (THE MAN BRINGS HER OVER) Listen to me, my daughter, do not fear--you are welcome here. Do not go to any other field to glean. You may come here and gather all you can and if you are thirsty, drink from the jars the men have filled.

Chorus: Assured was she of a safe surrounding,

> With gratitude her heart was
>   pounding.
> And when she told Naomi
>   where she had been,
> She learned that Boaz was
>   her next of kin.

SCENE IV: At Home

(RUTH AND NAOMI CAN BE STIRRING IN WOODEN BOWLS OR LOOKING OTHERWISE OCCUPIED)

Ruth: And he treated me so kindly--at first I was afraid but he assured me that no one would harm me--and that I should return.

Naomi: I have been wondering why Boaz has not called on us to see if he could help us. I suppose he has been busy--but now I know the stories of his greatness and his generosity are true.

Ruth: The other girls speak of how rich he is, that he is practically the head of the whole city! He doesn't have to be so kind--and yet he is. (THEY FREEZE IN POSITION AS THE CHORUS SPEAKS)

Chorus:
> Now ideas were rushing
>   through Naomi's head,
> Ruth needn't go gleaning--
>   she could marry instead,
> For she had the right as the
>   law then read,
> To ask her kin to take her
>   to wed.
> And insure by a child that

> *Kaddish* is said,
> For the husband she mourned
> --who lay in Moab--dead.

SCENE V: At Home

Naomi: Tonight after the harvest is finished, there will be a great party--eating and drinking and dancing--for everyone who worked. I want you to put on your best dress, fix your hair and perfume yourself--then go to the party.

Ruth: Why? What do you want me to do? I will do anything you ask--but I do not understand.

Naomi: Because Boaz is next of kin, you have the right to ask him to do what the law requires. I must sell my parcel of land since I cannot work it--and I need the money to live--and you need a husband to care for you--to give you a child.

Ruth: But Boaz? I don't know...he is so important. Why should he do this for me?

Naomi: I have seen the way he looks at you--and I have heard the way he speaks of you--he thinks you are special. I don't think he will mind at all.

Ruth: He is the kindest man I know--but how far will his kindness reach? After all, if we have a son, it really will not be his, but will belong to your son, my first husband--to carry on his name among our people--as you have told me.

Chorus: So Ruth went off as she was told,
Feeling nervous and somewhat bold.
And when Boaz awoke during the night,
His eyes beheld a surprising sight.
Afraid to disturb him and being discreet,
She was waiting silently at his feet.

He was greatly flattered at her request,
For of all the women--he thought her the best.
But someone was standing between Ruth and him,
Another relative who was closer in kin.
Boaz thought of a plan and told Ruth to wait,
And approached the man at the city gate.

SCENE VI: At the Gate

Boaz: Here--come here--it is I, your kinsman, Boaz! I must speak with you.

Man: Hello, Boaz. How are you? I hope your harvest was plentiful. What can I do for you?

Boaz: I have some business to discuss --I would like the elders of the city to stay to listen and bear witness. (AS BOAZ SAYS THIS IN THE DIRECTION OF THE CHORUS, THEY ALL COME UP ONTO THE STAGE AND GATHER AROUND REACTING TO THE SCENE) Do you remember the field that belonged to our kinsman, Elimelech?

Man: Yes--yes--a fine piece of land.

Boaz: Well, his widow, Naomi, wishes to sell. As the next of kin, it is your duty to buy this. If you don't want it, then I will help Naomi out and buy it.

Man: Oh--no--no--it is a good piece of land. No (AHEM) I mean, I should do what is right--after all, as the next of kin...

Boaz: Of course, you know, along with the property comes the daughter-in-law--the Moabitess, Ruth. She is in need of a husband--and a child to carry on the name of her poor dead husband.

Man: Oh--well--I don't know--spend my money on the land--and then it won't really even be mine--but will belong to the sons of Ruth! I--uh--I don't think so--no--I cannot do this!

Boaz: Don't worry, my friend--I will act as next of kin! You have all heard this--and are witness to it. I, Boaz, have accepted the duty of next of kin to Ruth, daughter-in-law of Naomi.

Chorus: Well, there was a wedding--

and joy of joys,
Ruth and Boaz had a baby boy.
He brought great happiness and when he grew,
He married and had a boy child, too!

And this child, Jesse, also had a son,
And he grew up to become number one.
And of this great-grandson of Ruth we sing,
His name was David-- a mighty King!

Amos, Man from Tekoah

Grades 7-12

PRODUCTION NOTES

The action of the play takes place in front of the Temple in Jerusalem during the time of Amos. The play can be performed as a pulpit presentation without scenery or on a stage with a more elaborate setting. The costumes can be modern dress or period. The ladies should be very overdressed and ostentatious.

AMOS, MAN FROM TEKOAH

CHARACTERS:

Yael	Timna
Shoshana	Elon
Oren	Mizzah
Ron	Amos
Eliphaz	Amaziah, the Priest
Zilpah	Vendor
Yurok	Servant

(THE SCENE OPENS WITH THE PLAYERS POSED IN GROUPS AS IF CAUGHT IN THE MIDST OF CONVERSATION. EACH GROUP BECOMES ACTIVATED AS IT BEGINS TO SPEAK.)

Ladies: (VERY SPOILED AND SNOBBISH SOUNDING)
    You can tell by looking at our clothes,
    By our jewels all sparkling,
    We are the upper class
    And we have everything.

Men: We're Israelites of the Northern Kingdom
    And Bethel is our city.
    We're rich and handsome and well dressed too,
    If you're not one of us, it's a pity.

All: And above all else, we're religious too.
    Don't you think that's good?

> And we offer sacrifices as
> we should.

Ron: How ya doin', Oren? How's business?

Oren: Things are pretty good. Of course, they could be better. Good help is so hard to find these days.

Eliphaz: I know what you mean. These days it takes three slaves to do the work of one.

Oren: And people ask why everything is getting more expensive—even the caravans are slowing down. There is so much thievery on the highways.

All: (CHANTING AGAIN AND MOVING, LEAVING ZILPAH, YUROK AND TIMNA CENTER STAGE)
> We are rich, we are rich,
> we are rich and good
> And we offer sacrifices as
> we should.

Zilpah: Yurok, darling, I love your dress. The material is fabulous. Who made it for you?

Yurok: Oh, it's really a rag. I hate it. I've worn it twice already and it bores me. I have to ask my husband for a new one.

Timna: I know what you mean, especially since the holidays are coming. I couldn't be seen at *Bethel* in a dress I've already worn.

Vendor: (CALLING FROM OFF STAGE THEN ENTERING) Jewelry, gold and

> We bring our offerings to the Temple
> Every time we should.

All: (CHANTING WHILE MOVING POSITIONS SO THAT SHOSHANA AND YAEL END UP CENTER STAGE)
> We are rich, we are rich,
> we are rich and good
> And we observe the sacrifices as we should.

Yael: Shoshana, my dear, how are you? I haven't seen you in so long! What have you been doing with yourself?

Shoshana: Oh, I've been so busy training a new slave.

Yael: Another new one? How many does that make for you? Your husband must be doing very well. Oh, I envy you. Your husband gives you everything.

Shoshana: Yes, he's doing quite well. He owns quite a bit of land and if the poor tenant can't pay his rent, well, then he sells us a member of his family. We're really doing them a favor. At least they know where their next meal is coming from. Frankly, I'm hoping a certain one can't pay. I've had my eye on his daughter. She'd make a wonderful serving girl.

All: (ALL CHANT AGAIN AS THEY MOVE, LEAVING OREN, RON AND ELIPHAZ CENTER STAGE)
> We are rich, we are rich,
> we are rich and good

precious stones from Phoenicia, Assyria and Egypt! See the beautiful jewels!

Ladies: Oh, let me see...me, too...I must have this...I want some, too...Wait, I saw that first...Come with me...I want my husband to see this...(ONE OF THE LADIES DRAGS THE VENDOR TO THE SIDE OF THE STAGE TO CONFER WITH HER HUSBAND. ALL THE REST OF THE LADIES FOLLOW ALONG SINGING TO THE TUNE OF "SWEET GYPSY ROSE" OR JUST SPEAKING:)

> Has anybody ever seen a ring sparkle so,
> A bracelet so bedazzling?
> Now we want to know,
> These rings on my fingers,
> I must make them mine.
> I'll buy again, cause she has ten and I have only nine!

Amos: (HAS ENTERED BEFORE THE SONG AND OBSERVED THE SCENE WITH THE VENDOR. NOW HE IS LEFT ALONE CENTER STAGE.)

> I can't believe what I hear,
> Their very words burn my ears,
> That they should be so selfish and greedy,
> They have no hearts, but oppress the needy.

Elon: How did you make out in court yesterday?

Mizzah: Oh, there was never any worry

...I gave the judge several pieces of gold and he dropped the charges.

Elon: And what about that ungrateful servant girl of yours, the one you thought stole your wife's jade necklace?

Mizzah: Oh, her. Well, actually it's very embarrassing. She was whipped and her servitude was extended to me for three more years...and then ...well, then I found the necklace ...it had fallen behind the ivory couch in my bedroom.

Amos: It angers me to hear their words,
That justice can be bought.
As Jews we should uphold what's right,
We were chosen for that,
I thought.

Servant: (RUNNING INTO ONE OF THE MEN) Master, I have searched everywhere. There is no more fabric for your wife's dress. The kind you have asked for has all been sold and the next caravan is not due in for a month.

Mizzah: You stupid idiot! You have not looked hard enough. There must be some! If Yurok has some, my wife must have some, too! Go and look some more, and if you come back without it, you'll get a beating!

Amos: (ALOUD TO THE PEOPLE)
Stop! I cannot bear to hear

             you speak.
             You think you're strong, but
                you're really weak.
             Like fat cows lying in the
                field,
             To the swift fox you'll
                someday yield.

Ladies: (ALL GASP)
          Who is this man?
          What does he say?
          He's mad to speak to us
             this way.
          Call Amaziah!
          Get the priest!
          We've got to get rid of this
             awful beast!

Amos: (AMAZIAH ENTERS AS AMOS BEGINS
   TO SPEAK)
             The Lord has told me that
                in turn,
             The Syrians, Ammonites and
                Moabites will burn.
             (ALL NOD)
             Their evil ways have angered
                the Lord,
             And so He will put them to
                the sword.

All: (APPLAUD) YES! YES!

Amos: But most of all, my fellow
                Jews,
             Oh, people of Israel, hear
                the news.
             You have forgotten what
                Moses has taught,
             All God's commandments have
                come to naught.
             And for your sins and evil

>
> ways,
> The Lord will end your
> prosperous days.

Amaziah: Stop! I have heard enough of this and of you! The news has come to me of a rabble-rouser roaming our cities and stirring up trouble. Return to your own land. There is no profit for a prophet here. We have no need of you or your blasphemous daydreams!

Amos:
> Don't you understand?
> Can't you see the light?
> You, of all these people
>   here,
> Don't you know what's right?
> You turn aside from justice,
> You forget to love,
> And now you shall be
>   destroyed from above!

Amaziah: You are not only a troublemaker, you are a traitor! You are frightening the people for no reason. I shall report you to the King. He will take care of you!

All: (AD-LIBS) Yes, tell the King. Did you hear what he said? The nerve of him. Who does he think he is? We certainly don't want his kind around.

Amos:
> You can take me to the King,
> But take heed of what I say.
> You shall all be conquered
>   and die unless
> You start to mend your way.

Ladies: He is mad, he is mad.

>   I will hear no more.
>   And his idle talk begins to bore.

Amaziah: You're coming with me! Seize this man! And follow me. We will take him to the King. He will dispose of this public nuisance once and for all. You will be silenced! You will learn! (TWO MEN GRAB AMOS AND DRAG HIM OUT FOLLOWING AMAZIAH)

All: (LAUGHING AND TWITTERING AS HE LEAVES THE STAGE...MUSIC UP AND SLOWLY BUILDING...BUYING BEGINS AGAIN FROM THE VENDOR...AS AMOS BEGINS TO SPEAK HIS FINAL SPEECH, ALL IS SILENT ON STAGE AND THE ACTION FREEZES)

Amos:
>   Take away the noise of your songs,
>   And let me not hear the melodies of your harps.
>   But let justice well up as waters,
>   And righteousness as a mighty stream!
>   (MUSIC UP AND OUT)

Home to Stay

Grades 7-12

PRODUCTION NOTES

Construct the Western Wall from cardboard boxes of varying sizes, stacked and painted to look like stone. If desired, place pieces of paper in the cracks so they can be seen by the audience. The costuming requirements are simple, with the possible exception of the uniforms. Perhaps a local little theatre group can loan uniforms to your group. Or you might borrow them from fathers or other individuals who have them stored away from their service days. If neither of these possibilities works out, use an assortment of hiking boots and khaki shirts and trousers.

HOME TO STAY

CHARACTERS:

    Boys from the Torah School

    Reporter

    Alon   - *A middle-aged soldier*

    Lavi   - *A young soldier*

    Two Women at the Wall

    Two Women Tourists

    Jeremiah

    Baruch

    Eleazar Ben Yair

    Soldiers at the Wall in '67

    An Old Arab

    Assorted Non-Speaking Parts in the Beginning Scene

(THE PLAY BEGINS IN TOTAL DARKNESS. FROM THE BACK OF THE AUDITORIUM, A GROUP OF BOYS WITH *TZITZIT* AND *KIPOT* ARE DRESSED IN MODERN SUMMER CLOTHING AND SANDALS. THEY BEGIN SINGING A SABBATH SONG WITH NO ACCOMPANIMENT. THEY MARCH TOGETHER DOWN THE AISLE IN A DOUBLE LINE, EACH WITH A HAND ON THE SHOULDER OF THE BOY AHEAD OF HIM. THEY WALK TO THE RHYTHM OF THE SONG THEY ARE SINGING. AS THEY APPROACH THE STAGE, THE CURTAINS OPEN REVEALING THE WALL AND MANY KINDS OF PEOPLE MILLING ABOUT--TOURISTS WITH CAMERAS

SNAPPING PICTURES, YOUNG SOLDIERS WITH RIFLES, OLD PEOPLE, CHILDREN, RELIGIOUS AND NON-RELIGIOUS INDIVIDUALS. THE YESHIVA STUDENTS COME UP ONTO THE STAGE AND FORM A HALF CIRCLE. AS THEY DO, THE PART OF THE CROWD THAT IS NOT ACTUALLY PRAYING, PARTS AND WATCHES AS THEY TAKE CENTER STAGE. THEY BEGIN TO DANCE, SWAYING WITH ARMS AROUND EACH OTHER'S SHOULDERS, AS THEY CONTINUE CHANTING A SONG. AS IT ENDS, THE BOYS DANCE OFF STAGE. ONE MAN IN A SPORT JACKET AND OPEN COLLARED SHIRT STEPS FORWARD WITH HIS HANDS IN HIS POCKETS. THE ENTIRE SCENE FREEZES AS HE BEGINS TO SPEAK.)

Reporter: It's hard for me to absorb all the changes. So much has happened since I was here last. So much growth around. When this area was opened to the Jews in '67, this was nothing more than an alleyway. Now...

Tourist: Excuse me, would you mind taking a picture of us in front of the Wall? (SHE HANDS HIM HER CAMERA AND SHE AND ANOTHER WOMAN STEP IN FRONT OF THE WALL AS THE REPORTER SNAPS THEIR PICTURE)

Reporter: No, not at all. Stand over there. (HE TAKES THE PICTURE AND HANDS THE CAMERA BACK)

Tourist: Thank you so much.

Tourist #2: It's our first trip, you

know. (THEY WALK AWAY)

Reporter: I can't get over it. They tore down the old dilapidated buildings that stood here and made this beautiful courtyard...and even the mood is different. It's as though people have always been coming here intoning their prayers...yet I remember so well another day, other feelings. I was here in Israel as a correspondent in June of '67, and I was standing almost on this same spot on the day Jerusalem was liberated. Such emotion gripped everyone! Such extraordinary happiness! No one could believe it. The barbed wire that had so unmercifully deprived the Jews of half their city for almost twenty years was down. There were mainly soldiers here then--soldiers like these with rifles slung on their backs. Only the soldiers were not clean and pressed. They had just survived seven of the most horrible days of their lives. (AT THE WALL ARE TWO SOLDIERS, ONE OBVIOUSLY OLDER THAN THE OTHER WHO WEARS A *TALLIT* AND *KIPAH*. THE YOUNGER ONE, LAVI, IS BAREHEADED. AN OLD MAN DRAPED IN A PRAYER SHAWL AND A FEW WOMEN ARE LEANING AGAINST THE WALL WITH THEIR BACKS TO THE AUDIENCE. THE OLDER SOLDIER, ALON, FINISHES HIS PRAYER, TUCKS A PIECE OF PAPER INTO ONE OF THE CRACKS AND TURNS AROUND. THE REPORTER APPROACHES HIM.)

Reporter: Excuse me.

Alon: *Kehn?*

Reporter: I wondered if I might talk to you for a moment?

Alon: How can I help you?

Reporter: I am an American Jew--a newspaper reporter, and I just wanted to get some feelings from people who live here about Jerusalem and the Wall belonging to Israel...what it means to you. Tell me, what would you sacrifice in the name of peace?

Alon: Well, let me tell you. I have grown up in this country, was born here even before it was a State. I live on a nearby *kibbutz*, and we have very--how do you say it --traditional beliefs.

Reporter: And your coming to the Wall ...how does that make you feel?

Alon: Feel? I still don't know if I'm feeling or dreaming each time I come here. You see, to me this city, Jerusalem, and this place, *HaKotel*, they are not things apart from me. They and I are one. It's like...like ...losing an arm and having it reattached again!

Reporter: (TO LAVI WHO HAS FINISHED HIS PRAYER AT THE WALL AND NOW MOVES IN TO JOIN THE CONVERSATION) How about you? Do you feel the same?

Lavi: I am not so religious, like Alon

here. I have never felt the need. We are all Jews here. I, too, was born here, but I have always known Israel as a State. But I have seen enough to know that we cannot take anything for granted.

Reporter: But if you are not as religious, why do you come to the Wall?

Lavi: (FINGERING THE STONES LOVINGLY) I can't tell you, exactly...I am overcome with a feeling of holiness. I look at these stones, I touch them--and I wonder... Here we are, moving freely about our city, able to express ourselves, to celebrate our holidays. There is concern, yes! But there is hope, too! Yet when I see this piece of Wall standing here, I can't help thinking what it must have been like for our people during the Destruction.

Woman I: (THE WOMEN HAVE FINISHED THEIR PRAYERS AND HAVE MOVED INTO THE DISCUSSION) I feel that time has stood still here in the Old City. I walked the narrow alleyways and thought to myself--this was the way the city looked hundreds of years ago.

Woman II: When I stand so close to these ancient stones, it is as if I can hear deep inside them the beating hearts of those who gave their lives for its defense.

Alon: It's like the song says, "There are men with hearts of stone; there are stones with hearts of men."

Woman I: But you can imagine what it must have been like to watch and wait like a trapped animal as the enemy approached, destroying all you loved--all you believed in. And then having your family split apart and dragged off in chains to be slaves!

Lavi: I can just imagine what it must have been like in the days of Jeremiah--the panic of the people as the Babylonians approached...

Woman II: ...hearing the prophecies of Jeremiah ringing in their ears as they were fulfilled.

(ON A RAISED PLATFORM DOWNSTAGE LEFT, A SPOTLIGHT FALLS ON THE LONE FIGURE OF A ROBED JEREMIAH. THE LIGHT OPENS WIDER TO INCLUDE THAT OF HIS DISCIPLE, BARUCH, SITTING IN FRONT OF HIM ON THE EDGE OF THE PLATFORM.)

Jeremiah: People are still streaming into the city, Baruch. They are still rushing to the Temple in hopes that their prayers will keep Nebuchadnezzar's armies away. Don't they know that only by casting away their sinful ways will the armies not come?

Baruch: This is the way of our people, Jeremiah. They hope that God will hear their prayers and halt the invasion of our country.

Jeremiah: Ah, but if a man put away his wife, and she go from him, and become another man's, may he return unto her again? So it is with Judah. They have embraced other gods, looked to other images, and now in their fear, they come calling God's name. But I have told them all along what would happen. I have begged them to repent of their sins, but no one would listen, and (VERY SADLY)...and now...

Baruch: Do not blame yourself, Jeremiah. It is not you who have failed. You did as God wished. You spoke the words He would have you say. It is the people who would not hear.

Jeremiah: Baruch, do you remember my prophecy? Do you remember the words I spoke to the people here at the Temple? Write them down. We will read them to the people again. Maybe it is not too late. Maybe this time they will listen. (JEREMIAH SITS DOWN NEXT TO BARUCH AND BEGINS TO RECOUNT HIS SPEECH. AS HE GETS CAUGHT UP IN WHAT HE IS SAYING, HE STANDS UP AGAIN AND CONTINUES TALKING IN AN IMPASSIONED MANNER.) Hear the word of the Lord, all ye of Judah, that enter in at these gates to worship the Lord. Amend your ways and your doings and I will cause you to dwell in this place. Be thou corrected, O Jerusalem, lest My soul be alienated from thee, lest I make thee desolate, a land not inhabited. For evil looketh from the north, and a great destruction. Behold, a people cometh from the north country, and a great nation shall be roused from the uttermost parts of the earth. They lay hold on bow and spear. They are cruel and have no compassion; their voice is like the roaring sea, and they ride upon horses; set in array, as a man for war, against thee, O daughter of Zion! (LIGHT OUT ON JEREMIAH AND UP ON THE REPORTER SCENE)

Woman II: How horrible it must have been when the Babylonians came. I've read in the Book of Jeremiah that they actually starved the people. The city finally fell when the bread supply gave out. The people were too weak to fight. Children were dying in their mother's arms and disease began to overtake the city.

Reporter: It's hard to imagine such a magnificent city totally destroyed —going up in flames like a scrap of paper!

Woman I: And the people, like you and me, marched off to be slaves!

Lavi: Now you can understand why the Zealots chose to isolate themselves on Masada during the Roman siege and eventually took their own lives instead of submitting to the Romans.

(LIGHTS GO OUT ON REPORTER AND UP ON A RAISED PLATFORM DOWNSTAGE RIGHT, REVEALING A ROBED FIGURE OF ELEAZAR BEN YAIR, THE LEADER OF THE ZEALOTS)

Ben Yair: My friends, we are all gathered here for one purpose. We swore long ago that we would never be taken slaves of the Romans. Many of us were the first to defy them when they first entered our beloved city. Even as we stand talking, our city is being destroyed around us and our Temple is in danger. We all know that it is only a matter of days now before the Romans will overwhelm us all. My dear friends, it is time to put our plan into action. God has given us a chance to rob them of their victory. Let us not wait around to see our women ravaged, our children tortured and ourselves tormented until our spirit is broken. Go home. Pack what you need. Gather your families and let us proceed to Masada in the way we have planned. And if we must die, it will be with the love of God on our lips and the love of freedom in our hearts! (BLACKOUT ON BEN YAIR AND LIGHTS BACK UP ON THE REPORTER SCENE)

Woman II: It's as though every time I put my ear close to these stones, I can hear a heart beating deep inside.

Alon: I'm sure it's hard for a non-

Jew to understand why this Wall should be so important to us. After all, it's only stone. But to me, to many of us, it's more than that—it's our history. It's our identity with the greatness of ages past. It's a reminder of the Destruction and of what could happen again if we choose to forget God's teachings. We feel so close to Him here that we actually slip notes to Him in the cracks.

Woman I: Freedom! That is what this Wall symbolizes! Freedom to be Jews!

Alon: I was a soldier in the unit that got to the Wall first back in '67. It was incredible. I remember it as if it were yesterday. It was Wednesday. We found ourselves wandering in the narrow, winding streets not really knowing where we were or if we would at any minute be the victim of a sniper's bullet. It had been a good twenty years since any Jew had been inside the Old City. We found an old Arab to lead us to the Wall.

(AS HE CONTINUES HIS MONOLOGUE, ACTORS DEPICTING THE SOLDIERS AND THE OLD ARAB COME DOWN THE CENTER AISLE FROM THE BACK OF THE AUDITORIUM IN THE DARKENED ROOM INTERSPERSING THEIR OWN DIALOGUE. IT IS POSSIBLE TO "DOUBLE CAST" AND USE SOME OF THE TORAH STUDENTS AS MALE AND FEMALE SOLDIERS.)

Soldier I: (IN A HUSHED VOICE) Do you know where we are going?

Arab: Thees way. You follow me.

Soldier II: I don't know where we are. I feel like we've been going in circles.

Soldier I: Look! There! That's it. That's the Wall! (THE SOLDIERS LEAP UP ONTO THE STAGE, HUGGING EACH OTHER AND, PLACING THEIR HEADS AGAINST THE STONES, RUB THEIR HANDS LOVINGLY ACROSS THEM. THEY SEEM AS IF THEY ARE WEEPING. THEY FREEZE INTO THIS POSE AS ALON CONTINUES HIS MONOLOGUE.)

Alon: The *Kotel* had seen all kinds of people over the years, but never before had it seen bloodstained, weeping paratroopers. I stood there with the tears streaming down my face. One of our men had a flag with him and had made his way to the top of the Wall. (ONE OF THE SOLDIERS HAS GONE BEHIND THE WALL OF BOXES AND CLIMBED A STEP LADDER WHICH ALLOWS HIM TO BE SEEN AT THE TOP OF THE WALL. HE HANGS AN ISRAELI FLAG OVER THE BOXES.)

Soldier III: (SHOUTING AS THE FLAG IS PLACED) It's ours! Jerusalem is ours once again! (HE DISAPPEARS LEAVING THE FLAG IN VIEW. THE REPORTER SCENE ONCE AGAIN ASSUMES CENTER STAGE.)

Alon: You see, emotion overwhelmed us because we had finally undone what had happened almost two thousand years ago.

Woman I: For the first time since the Roman Destruction, Jerusalem and all her holy places are open to everyone. We can all come and worship freely now that these sites belong to Israel once again.

Lavi: And I know that even though I was too young to fight in '67 and '73, and though I had no part in liberating the Wall, I wouldn't hestate to give my life to defend it just as our people were forced to do in other times.

Alon: And there's something else we know in our hearts. On Tisha B'Av, when we take off our shoes and sit on the ground by the Wall and read Lamentations and weep and mourn, we mourn only for the past. For Israel has finally come home and we are here to stay!

(DURING THIS LAST SPEECH, *HATIKVAH* CAN BE PLAYING SOFTLY IN THE BACKGROUND. WHEN THE SPEECH ENDS, THE SPOTLIGHT IS LEFT ON THE FLAG AS THE MUSIC IS BROUGHT UP, OVER AND OUT. A BLACKOUT SHOULD OCCUR AS THE MUSIC ENDS.)

Bibliography

BIBLIOGRAPHY

Books About Drama/Books of Plays

Assembly Playlets for Day Schools and Afternoon Schools. N.Y.: Torah Umesorah Publications.

Barnfield, Gabriel. *Creative Drama in Schools.* N.Y.: Hart Publishing Co., 1968.

Citron, Samuel. *Dramatics for Creative Teaching.* N.Y.: United Synagogue of America, 1961.

_____. *Dramatics the Year Round.* N.Y.: United Synagogue of America, 1956.

_____. *Israel--Dream and Fulfillment.* N.Y.: Jewish Education Committee Press, 1968.

Dramatics for the Jewish Club Leader. N.Y.: Yeshiva University, Dept. of Youth Services, Division of Communal Services.

Gabriel, Michelle. *Jewish Plays for Jewish Days: Brief Holiday Plays for Ages 8-12.* Denver: Alternatives in Religious Education, Inc., 1978.

Goodrich, Frances and Hackett, Albert. *The Diary of Anne Frank.* N.Y.: Random House, 1956.

Goodridge, Janet. *Creative Drama and

Improvised Movement for Children. Boston: Plays, Inc., 1970.

Howard, Vernon. *Pantomime, Charades and Skits.* N.Y.: Sterling Publishing Co., 1974.

Johnson, Richard C. "Producing Plays for Children," in *The Theatre Student.* N.Y.: Richards Rosen Press, Inc., 1971.

Klein, Joyce. "Drama in the Jewish Classroom," in *The Jewish Teachers Handbook.* Edited by Audrey Friedman Marcus. Denver: Alternatives in Religious Education, Inc., 1980.

Lepkin, Bela. *Creative Drama in the Hebrew School.* N.Y.: Bloch Publishing Co., 1978.

McCaslin, Nellie. *Creative Dramatics in the Classroom.* N.Y.: David McKay, 1974.

Rembrandt, Elaine. "Educational Theatre in the Religious School," in *The Jewish Teachers Handbook,* Volume II. Edited by Audrey Friedman Marcus. Denver: Alternatives in Religious Education, Inc., 1981.

Schwardelson, Susan J. *Kadima Drama Manual.* N.Y.: United Synagogue of America, Dept. of Youth Activities.

Wyenn, Than R. *Parallel Dramatics.* Los Angeles: Bureau of Jewish Education.

Wykell, Esther. *Creative Dramatics in the Jewish School*. Chicago: Board of Jewish Education, 1962.

Sources for Scripts

American Zionist Youth Foundation, 515 Park Ave., New York, NY 10022.

Anti-Defamation League, 823 United Nations Plaza, New York, NY 10017.

B'nai B'rith, Dept. of Adult Jewish Education, 1640 Rhode Island Ave. N.W., Washington, DC 20036.

B'nai B'rith Youth Organization, 1640 Rhode Island Ave. N.W., Washington, DC 20036.

Dramatists Play Service, 440 Park Ave., New York, NY 10016.

Gil Aberg, 704 McKee St., State College, PA 16801.

Habonim, 575 Sixth Ave., New York, NY 10009.

Hadassah Education Dept., 50 West 58th St., New York, NY 10017.

Hadassah Zionist Youth Commission, 717 Broadway, New York, NY 10003.

Jewish Education Press, 426 West 58th St., New York, NY 10019.

Jewish National Fund, 42 East 69th St.,

New York, NY 10021.

Jewish Theological Seminary, Dept. of Radio and Television, 3080 Broadway, New York, NY 10027.

Jewish Welfare Board, 15 East 26th St., New York, NY 10010.

National Council for Jewish Women, 15 East 26th St., New York, NY 10010.

National Foundation for Jewish Culture, 122 East 42nd St., New York, NY 10017.

Samuel French, Inc., 25 West 45th St., New York, NY 10036.

Torah Umesorah Publications, 229 Park Ave. South, New York, NY 10003.

Yeshiva University, Dept. of Youth Services, Division of Communal Services, 500 West 185th St., New York, NY 10033.

Bibliographies of Plays

Cohen, Edward, Editor. *Plays of Interest: A Preliminary Catalogue.* N.Y.: Jewish Theatre Association. Available from the National Foundation for Jewish Culture, 122 East 42nd St., Suite 1512, New York, NY 10068.

Goodman, Hannah Grad. *An Annotated and Selected Bibliography of Dramatic Scripts on American Jewish Themes.* N.Y.: Jewish Book Council of the Jewish Welfare Board, 1975.